Property-Casualty Principles

Property and Casualty Continuing Education Course

At press time, this edition contains the most complete and accurate information currently available. Owing to the nature of license examinations, however, information may have been added recently to the actual test that does not appear in this edition. Please contact the publisher to verify that you have the most current edition.

This publication is designed to provide accurate and authoritative information in regard to the subject matter covered. It is sold with the understanding that the publisher is not engaged in rendering legal, accounting, or other professional services. If legal advice or other expert assistance is required, the services of a competent professional should be sought.

We value your input and suggestions. If you found imperfections or incorrect information in this product, please let us know by sending an email to **errata@kaplan.com**.

We are always looking for ways to make our products better to help you achieve your career goals.

PROPERTY-CASUALTY PRINCIPLES, 3RD EDITION
©2006 DF Institute, Inc., d/b/a Kaplan Financial Education. All rights reserved.

The text of this publication, or any part thereof, may not be reproduced in any manner whatsoever without written permission from the publisher.

Published by DF Institute, Inc., d/b/a Kaplan Financial Education.

Printed in the United States of America.

ISBN: 1-4195-8087-6

PPN: 5392-8901

06	**07**	**10**	**9**	**8**	**7**	**6**	**5**	**4**	**3**	**2**	**1**
J	F	M	A	M	J	**J**	A	S	O	N	D

Contents

Introduction v

UNIT 1 How We All Benefit from Insurance 1

How Insurance Helps People 2   Looking Ahead 11

UNIT 2 General Concepts of Insurance 13

What Risk Is 14   Risk and Insurance 18

UNIT 3 An Overview of the Insurance Industry 35

Major Branches of Insurance 36   Insurance Regulation 46

Types of Insurance Companies 41   The Government as an Insurer 54

UNIT 4 The People Behind the Promise 55

Marketing 57   Claims 77

Underwriting 64   Other Insurance Functions 81

Rating, Rates, and Premiums 71   Teams 85

Policy Issue/Administration/
Service 77

UNIT 5 The Insurance Contract 87

Characteristics of Contracts 88   Declarations 98

Standardization of Policies 90   Insuring Agreement 100

Classifications of Policies 91   Exclusions 104

Sections of a Policy 94   Conditions 105

UNIT 6   Property-Casualty Insurance Policies   117

Personal Lines Policies   118

Commercial Lines Policies   128

UNIT 7   Improving Understanding of Insurance   145

Why Insurance Isn't Readily Understood   146

Questions People Often Ask About Insurance   148

Doing Something About It   147

Review Test   157

Glossary   175

Index   183

Introduction

Welcome to the world of insurance! You'll soon discover—if you haven't already—that it's an exciting industry. It's exciting because:

- It's a busy place. It takes a lot of people doing many different types of jobs to make it all work. And every person's contribution is needed. No matter what job you have in the insurance industry, it's an important one.

- It's a growing place. Although insurance has been around a long time, the industry continues to find ways to serve its customers better. In the days and years to come, there will continue to be new things to learn about this business.

There's so much to know about insurance that you may even feel a little overwhelmed right now—but don't worry. This book will give you an easy-to-understand overview of everything you need to know to get off to a good start.

In this course, you'll learn:

- How insurance serves the public
- The roles played by various people in the insurance business
- What some basic insurance terms mean
- The parts of the typical insurance policy
- Which policies cover what types of losses
- The answers to some frequently asked questions about insurance

WHO SHOULD STUDY THIS COURSE

There is no course you need to study first in order to understand the material in this one. This course is designed as orientation training for new employees in any area of the property-casualty insurance business.

After you take this course, you'll want to continue your study of insurance. Among your options for further study, you or your supervisor may choose from a number of our courses on general insurance topics such as ethics, communication, or other skills. We also offer specialized training for individuals in claims, underwriting, and rating, as well as a wide range of courses on various coverages available to individuals and businesses.

HOW TO USE THIS COURSE

Programmed Instruction

As you proceed through each unit of *Property-Casualty Principles*, you'll have the opportunity to interact with the study material and check your progress. This method of learning is called **programmed instruction.** Each step in programmed instruction is numbered for your easy reference. Each of these numbered steps is called a **frame,** and a series of frames comprises a **unit.**

To learn more about how programmed instruction works, read the frames that follow and respond as requested.

1. Three of the basic principles of programmed instruction are:

    1. The material is presented step-by-step, in logical groupings.

    2. After you have read an increment of information, you are asked to demonstrate your comprehension and retention of what you've learned by answering questions, selecting the correct answer from a number of options or by responding to the information in some other way.

    3. You receive immediate confirmation of your response. The answers and suggestions provided in the textbook are located immediately below the frame exercise.

    Now, try this exercise.

    Each of the following statements corresponds to one of the three principles we just listed. Mark a **1, 2** or **3** in front of each statement to match it to the principle it represents.

    ____ A. Throughout the course, you will apply what you have learned by answering questions.

    ____ B. You will know each step of the way whether you have understood the material up to that point.

    ____ C. The text takes you through the material step-by-step, in logical groupings.

    Answer: 2 A.; 3 B.; 1 C.

2. You should check your answer after completing each frame in the text.

   If your answer matches the printed answer that immediately follows the exercise, go to the next frame. If it does not match, review the material in the frame, then respond differently. Check that response. You may need to follow this procedure more than once in a single frame. If the correct response still escapes you, read the material again from the beginning. Such review is more likely to be necessary if there has been a prolonged interruption in your study.

   If the response you have made does not match the response that appears after the exercise, you should first
   A. go on to the next frame
   B. go back several frames and start over
   C. review the material in the frame and select a different response

   Answer: C is correct.

3. Once you understand the material in a frame, go to the next frame and repeat the study-respond-verify cycle.

   Arrange the following steps in the correct sequence by writing a number in the blank beside each statement to indicate how to proceed through a programmed instruction text. Write **1** for the first step, **2** for the second step, and so on.
   ____ A. Check your response.
   ____ B. Read the material in the frame.
   ____ C. Go to the next frame.
   ____ D. Answer the question asked in the frame.
   ____ E. Repeat the previous steps until you understand, reading the prior material again if necessary.

   Answer: 3 A.; 1 B.; 5 C.; 2 D.; 4 E.

Other Features of Programmed Instruction

4. Programmed instruction incorporates some other features that will make your study even more effective:

   - **Illustrations**: The course includes illustrations, charts and graphics to stimulate your interest in what you are studying, make concepts easier to understand and promote retention of what you have learned.

   - **Key Words**: Pay special attention to terms that are in **boldface** type. It is important that you know the meanings of these key words.

- **Job Builders**: Occasionally, the Notes column on a page will contain instructions for you to perform some job-related activity. These activities may help you directly relate what you have learned to your job. Although your supervisor may review the results of those activities, you will *not* be tested on them on the examination you will take when you have completed this course.

Which of the following statements concerning programmed instruction are correct?

A. Illustrations are often used to explain certain concepts more effectively.
B. It is important that you know the meaning of key words printed in boldface type.
C. The course exam includes questions on the results of Job Builder activities.

Answer: A and B are correct.

When you've completed the course, you will take a multiple choice review test at the end of the book. If you work through the course carefully, you should do well on the exam.

When you're ready, start your study with Unit One.

1
How We All Benefit from Insurance

1. In this unit, you will become acquainted with the many ways in which people benefit from insurance. This unit will show you how insurance:

   - gives financial stability to policyholders and their families,
   - helps communities prosper, and
   - contributes to our economy as an employer, taxpayer, and investor.

   For you to grasp the importance of your work, you need to understand these contributions.

HOW INSURANCE HELPS PEOPLE

Insurance Helps People Stay Financially Stable

2. In a very obvious and personal way, insurance makes life better. People who buy insurance gain some very valuable benefits in terms of financial stability and in the form of help in recovering from and preventing losses and in obtaining credit. Let's look first at the benefit of financial stability.

   Think of the financial consequences that you (and everyone else) could face without insurance. Say you have an accident on your way to work tomorrow and damage your car extensively. Could you pay a $5,000 repair bill right now? Or, if your home or apartment should burn down today, could you easily come up with the thousands of dollars you'd need to rebuild and buy new furniture and personal effects? If you're like most of us, that would be really tough, if not impossible; it could be disastrous.

   But let's look at the bright side. With your car and your home or apartment insured, you'll get your money back for those losses. So, however unfortunate events such as these may be in other ways, your finances won't be drained, and you and your family's financial stability won't be undermined. You'll be able to keep your present lifestyle, and your future plans—to buy a newer car or a more expensive home, to send your children to college, to enjoy a comfortable retirement—can remain intact.

Benefit of Insurance

Property-Casualty insurance protects people against many of life's perils.

In which of the following instances have people benefited because they owned insurance? (Check all that apply.)

A. After a tornado destroys the Albert family home, their insurance company pays to have it rebuilt exactly as it used to be on the same lot.

B. Thieves break the window on Lisa Smith's car and steal her factory-installed CD player; the insurance company pays for the damage to the car, including a new CD player.

C. Tim Harper loses control of his car while driving and strikes John Taylor, a pedestrian. John is disabled and sues Tim for his medical expenses, a lifetime of lost wages, and pain and suffering. The insurance company pays John's claim against Tim.

Answer: A, B, and C are correct.

Insurance Helps Communities Prosper

Help in Recovering from Ordinary Losses

3. People can benefit from insurance even if they don't own it themselves. In fact, everyone benefits from insurance.

   Here's an example. A fire destroys a local business. The business isn't insured, so the owners could lose everything. A lot of people depended on that business. If it no longer exists:

   ■ the employees will lose their jobs;

   ■ the business's suppliers will lose money and may have to cut back its their own workforce or drop its plans for expansion;

   ■ the community will lose tax revenues that the business and its employees were paying. Those funds now won't be available for essential government services such as water and sewer, fire protection, and police protection;

   ■ customers won't be able to buy the business's products or services. If the business supplied essential components to other businesses, those businesses may have to curtail their operations.

   If the business is insured, however, these losses can be avoided. The business can be rebuilt quickly, people can get back to work, and the flow of economic activity from that business can resume.

Everybody Wins with Insurance

Unit 1 How We All Benefit from Insurance 5

Besides the owners of the business, who regain their investment and their livelihood, name at least three parties who benefit from insurance on a business when it suffers an insured loss, and describe how they benefit.

employees - keep their jobs
suppliers - keep their business/revenues
community - regains tax rev
customers - regain service

Answer: Employees regain their jobs; suppliers regain their business revenues; community regains its tax revenues; customers regain essential products or services (any three, any order).

Help Recovering from Catastrophic Losses

4. We've discussed the "ripple effect" that the loss of a single business can have. Now think of the long-term and widespread devastation caused by events such as hurricanes or earthquakes. Imagine the losses that would result from those catastrophes if there were no such thing as insurance. It would take many years for areas of the country to rebuild after a natural disaster if it weren't for the revitalizing power of the insurance money paid to cover those losses. Meanwhile a region would sink into an economic slump, and even cause a drag on the economy of the nation as a whole.

Another Reason for Insurance

Insurance helps communities rebuild after catastrophes.

Because hurricanes, earthquakes, and other natural catastrophes are so highly publicized, the way the insurance industry responds to such events has a big impact on how people perceive the insurance industry. For example, when Hurricane Andrew virtually destroyed large areas of south Florida and coastal Louisiana in 1992, insurers began sending in teams even as the winds subsided. With power and telephone lines downed and roads blocked, adjusters made extraordinary, round-the-clock efforts to contact insureds who had suffered losses. Insurance companies made special arrangements with the small number of banks that were still operating in those areas to cash the claim checks written to their insureds. This quick and caring response earned praise from insureds, the media, and even the President of the United States.

While this particular example of the insurance industry's responsiveness earned a great deal of publicity, it's important to remember that every loss—even if it isn't particularly newsworthy—is *somebody's* catastrophe. It's the insurance industry's job to make a quick and caring response not just in extraordinary circumstances but also for the isolated losses that occur to individual insureds every day.

As a member of the insurance industry, the work you do instantly impacts other people's lives. Whether you work directly with the public or not, your job plays an important role in the service your company provides to its customers. (We'll go into more detail on the essential roles various individuals play in the insurance process in Unit Four.)

So take pride in your work and in this industry. The teams sent into Florida and Louisiana after Hurricane Andrew provided relief to hundreds of thousands of people, *but they did so one person at a time*. You can have the same sort of impact with each of the individuals you interact with in the course of your job. No matter what role you play, keep the ultimate effect on the customer in mind. Making your efforts the best they can be will help ensure that insurance will continue to have a positive impact on everyone.

Select the correct statement.

A. The primary contribution the insurance industry makes to the well-being of the public is in its response to natural disasters, such as hurricanes.

B. The only people in the insurance industry who make a contribution to the well-being of the public are those who deal directly with it.

C. Anyone involved in the insurance industry can make an important contribution to the well-being of the public every day by doing the best job possible.

Answer: C is correct.

Preventing Losses

5. The insurance industry is constantly working to prevent losses from occurring. In fact, insurance loss prevention activities in North America date back to colonial times.

    Benjamin Franklin formed the first fire insurance company in the United States in 1752. He then organized efforts to educate people about the ways they could keep their homes free of fire. He invented two things that help reduce the incidence of house fires: the lightning rod and the Franklin stove. And, he established Philadelphia's first volunteer fire department.

    Insurance companies continue this tradition today. In addition to insuring businesses, they employ **loss control specialists** and **engineers** to inspect a business's premises and make appropriate recommendations for improving workplace safety and for preventing crime, fire, or other **perils** (a peril is anything that causes a loss). Some businesses buy insurance as much to obtain loss prevention services as for the insurance coverage. Some insurance companies also encourage loss prevention by offering discounts to insureds who have certain safety equipment or fire or crime prevention devices installed in their homes, cars, or businesses.

Loss Prevention

Insurance companies try to prevent losses, too.

Insurance industry trade associations and groups of companies contribute funds to many organizations that promote safe products, safe workplaces and safety in the home and on the road. Organizations devoted to preventing fires and many types of crime also receive funds from insurance industry sources.

Insurance industry groups participate in campaigns to raise public awareness about safety and crime prevention and to enact legislation to reduce hazards such as drunken driving.

Loss prevention contributes greatly to the quality of our lives since it spares us not only financial loss but also the accompanying physical and emotional suffering from events such as an accidental injury or the loss of a home or other property to fire, criminal act, or other peril.

Which of the following are ways the insurance industry helps prevent losses?

A. A national association of insurance companies donates $20,000 to the National Safety Council.
B. XYZ Insurance Company sends an engineer to inspect the steam boilers and other machinery at ABC Company, a prospective insured.
C. DEF Insurance Company offers a 10% premium discount on fire coverage to homeowners who have smoke alarms, fire extinguishers, and dead bolts installed in their homes.
D. LMN Insurance Company pays a $10,000 auto insurance claim for collision damage sustained to an auto.

Answer: A, B, and C are correct. D illustrates recovery after a loss, an important function of insurance but not a loss prevention activity.

Insurance Helps People Obtain Credit

6. Being able to obtain credit is essential if our economy is to flourish. Without credit, most people couldn't buy homes or cars or make other major purchases, and without demand for those products, our economic engine would stall. Without credit, most businesses couldn't start, much less expand, their operations, and many jobs simply wouldn't be created. Without jobs, people wouldn't have the money to buy goods and services. Credit improves the quality of life and makes it possible for people to obtain many goods and services sooner than would be possible if they had to pay cash for them.

   How does insurance fit into the credit system? An example will help explain. Let's say you want to buy a house. It costs $50,000. You only have $10,000, so you borrow $40,000 from a bank. The $40,000 loan gives the bank a **financial interest** in your house. That is, in order to help ensure that you can pay back the $40,000, the bank wants to make sure that nothing happens to your house. What if your house burned down? The bank would lose $40,000!

   When it lends you the money, then, the bank will ask you to insure your house. The policy will be written so that if the house is destroyed, the bank will be paid the amount of its financial interest in the house, which will decrease as you make payments on your loan. You will receive the balance of the benefits. The insurance policy protects the bank against loss. The same principle works to help people get car loans and to help businesses get money to expand. Insurance works hand in hand with credit to maintain our nation's prosperity and standard of living.

Insurance and the Credit System

Insurance protects lenders as well as owners.

Keri purchases a $20,000 car, using $5,000 of her own money and a $15,000 bank loan. She has the car insured. While she is driving the car home from the dealership, it collides with another car. No one is hurt, but her new car is destroyed. Who will receive insurance benefits under Keri's policy?

A. Keri only
B. The bank only
C. Both Keri and the bank
D. The car dealer

Answer: C is correct.

7. Besides the benefits we've just discussed, the insurance industry has a major impact on the nation's economic well-being in the following areas:

- ***As an employer***: Insurance companies, agencies, and service organizations employ over 2,500,000 individuals in various capacities. Every year, these individuals earn a total of more than $100 billion. Another half million people are employed by companies that supply the computers, office equipment, and other goods and services the insurance industry needs to conduct business.

- ***As a taxpayer***: The insurance industry is a major source of revenue for both the federal government and the individual states. Premium taxes paid to the states total nearly $8 billion a year. The amount of income taxes paid to the federal government fluctuates depending on changes in tax rules and operating results, but the figure for property-casualty insurance companies alone has ranged between $1.5 billion and nearly $5 billion in recent years.

- **As an investor**: Without the investments made by the insurance industry, private companies and governments at all levels would have a harder time finding the money required to finance their operations. The insurance industry has over $2.5 trillion invested in the public and private sectors of the economy. Of that amount, about $500 billion is invested in U.S. government securities, and over $225 billion is invested in state and local government securities. Over $1 trillion is invested in corporate securities, with the remainder in other types of investments, such as real estate and money market instruments.

Ask your supervisor how many people your company employs. Ask for a copy of your company's latest annual report and see how much money your company paid in taxes and how much it has invested in the economy. This information will help you appreciate the role your company plays in the economy as an employer, a taxpayer, and an investor.

Match the specific examples of the ways insurance helps people at the left with the general categories listed on the right.

_4_ A. XYZ Insurance Company's loss control specialist makes several recommendations designed to reduce the incidence of workplace accidents at a client company.

_1_ B. Karen's insurance company pays her $120,000 to have her home rebuilt after it is destroyed by a tornado.

_2_ C. John is able to go back to work only two weeks after a fire damages his employer's manufacturing company.

_8_ D. ABC Insurance Company purchases a large number of bonds issued by a municipal school corporation.

_6_ E. Janine has worked for the DEF Insurance Company for over 20 years.

_7_ F. A state collects over $40 million in premium taxes in one year.

_3_ G. After a hurricane, insurance companies send in teams to settle claims.

_5_ H. Jerry is able to get a loan to purchase a new car after obtaining adequate collision coverage.

1. Financial security for insureds
2. Restoring economic stability after ordinary losses
3. Restoring economic stability after catastrophic losses
4. Loss prevention
5. Allows extension of credit
6. Major employer
7. Major taxpayer
8. Major investor

Answer: 4 A.; 1 B.; 2 C.; 8 D.; 6 E.; 7 F.; 3 G.; 5 H.

LOOKING AHEAD

Many members of the public aren't aware of the contributions insurance makes to the well being of individuals and society or don't understand the workings of this complex product. At the end of this course, we will deal with some of the questions that you may hear people ask, or that you may have. Before we can answer them, however, we need to present some technical concepts relating to insurance. In the next unit, we will discuss why insurance was developed and the principles on which insurance is based.

UNIT 2

General Concepts of Insurance

1. In this unit, you will become acquainted with some of the fundamental concepts of insurance. This unit will explain:

    - how insurance helps individuals manage some of the risks of life,
    - the factors that determine whether a risk can be insured, and
    - what the "principle of indemnity" is and how it relates to insurance.

    Knowing these concepts sets the stage for learning more about the insurance industry and the products it sells.

WHAT RISK IS

2. The purpose of insurance is to help people manage **risk**. According to one definition, risk is the *possibility of loss*. For our purposes, we will limit the definition somewhat further:

Risk

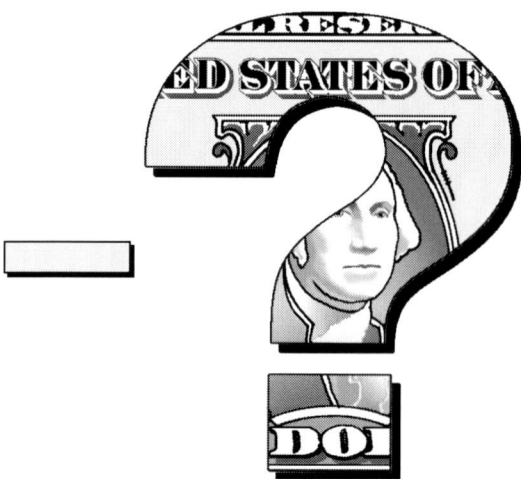

Risk is uncertainty about financial loss.

Which of the following involves risk?
A. John pays $25 toward the balance on his gasoline credit card.
B. Mary throws a silver dollar into a wishing well.
C. Ted, in slippery shoes, is carrying a valuable cut-glass antique vase across a smooth, wet concrete floor.

Answer: Only C is correct. In A, no financial loss occurs because the money is given in return for value already received. In B, money is lost, but it's done intentionally, so there's no uncertainty regarding the loss. In C, uncertainty exists as to whether Ted will get across the floor with the vase intact. He might not fall, or he might fall without breaking the vase, but if he slips and drops the vase, a financial loss will occur. This meets our definition of risk.

3. The possibility of loss is not measurable—it either exists or it doesn't. When we begin to talk about measuring the likelihood of a loss actually occurring, we are dealing with a different concept called **probability**. The *probability of loss* is sometimes also referred to as risk.

   A loss that is unlikely to occur, such as hurricane damage to a home in the Colorado Rockies, has a probability approaching zero. A loss that is certain to occur, such as milk spoiling when it is left unrefrigerated, has a probability of one. All potential losses can be rated on a scale of zero to one, according to the likelihood that they will occur. A loss that is more likely to occur gets a higher rating (closer to a "1") than a loss that is less likely to occur (and gets a rating closer to "0").

   Rate the following potential losses on the scale shown.
   A. Falling off a bridge by noon tomorrow
   B. Getting sick and missing work at some point in your career

   Scale of Likelihood

   0 ―――――――――――――――――――――――――――― 1

   Answer:
   0   A   B   1

4. In addition to the possibility of loss and the probability of loss, insurance people sometimes use the term "risk" to refer to the *subject of insurance*.

   Bill purchases a motorcycle and has it insured. Using "risk" in the sense we have just discussed, what is the risk in this situation? _____
   _____
   _____

   Answer: The motorcycle

Three Types of Risk

5. Speaking again of risk as the possibility of loss, risks fall into three broad classifications:

   ■ ***Personal risk***: This is the possibility that something will happen to you personally that would create a financial loss for you. For example, if you were seriously injured in an accident, you would have to go to the doctor, or perhaps even the hospital. Having to pay the bills from these medical care providers would represent a financial loss to you.

- **Property risk**: This is the risk that something will happen to your property that will result in a financial loss to you. For example, if you ran off the road and hit a tree while you were driving your auto, it would likely result in some damage to it. Having to pay to get your auto repaired would represent a financial loss to you.

- **Liability risk**: This is the risk that you will be found legally responsible for paying for losses incurred by someone else. In such a case, the other person's damages become your financial loss. For example, if you were driving your auto and it collided with a truck, the truck as well as your auto would probably be damaged, and you and other people might be injured. If you were found legally responsible for the accident, having to pay the other persons' medical care and car repair bills would represent a financial loss to you.

Classify each of the following as involving personal, property, or liability risk.

A. After sprinkling your lawn, you leave your garden hose lying dangerously across your front steps. A visitor trips over the hose, falls, and breaks an arm. _____

B. You are standing at the top of a ladder, painting the side of your house and leaning way over to reach a corner. _____

C. You forget to turn off a burner on your gas stove before you leave the house for work. A breeze wafts the kitchen curtains toward the open flame. _____

Answer: A. Liability; B. Personal; C. Property

Managing Risk

6. People have developed several methods of managing risk.

Risk Management Methods

There are four methods of handling risk.

One method is simply to **avoid** risk. You can avoid the risk of being in a plane crash by never getting on a plane, for example.

But it isn't practical to avoid all risks. Fortunately, that isn't the only method of managing risk. You can also **control** risk to some extent. For example, training workers in the safe use of welding tools can curtail the frequency of fires on the job. Risk control techniques that curtail the frequency of losses come under the heading of **loss prevention**. Or, installing a sprinkler system in a factory won't prevent a fire from occurring, but it will limit the severity of any fire that does occur. Risk control techniques that limit the severity of losses come under the heading of **risk reduction**.

In some cases, people simply **retain** a risk. That is, if any loss occurs, they will pay for it themselves. Sometimes people retain only a portion of a risk—the portion that remains after other means of managing the risk have been employed. If people are aware of a risk and decide to retain it (or a portion of it), then they do so intentionally. If people are not aware of a risk, they may retain it unintentionally, and they may be surprised if a loss occurs.

The final method of managing risk is to **transfer** it. The most common method of transferring risk is insurance. By purchasing a policy, the insured transfers certain risks to the insurance company. If a loss occurs, the insurance company, rather than the insured, pays it.

The transaction isn't just as simple as that, of course, but that's the essential idea. In the rest of this course—and in your insurance career—you'll be learning a lot more about what is involved in transferring risk through insurance.

Match the description at left with the method of managing risk at right.

____ A. George always wears his seat belt in the car.

____ B. Terry has no collision coverage on her car.

____ C. Heidi insures her $10,000 diamond bracelet for its full value.

____ D. Dale refuses to drink if he'll be driving, and refuses to drive if he's been drinking.

1. Avoid risk
2. Control risk
3. Retain risk
4. Transfer risk

Answer: 2 A.; 3 B.; 4 C.; 1 D.

RISK AND INSURANCE

Definition of Insurance

7. **Insurance** is a device that allows the losses that occur to a relatively small number of people to be shared among the members of a large group. When people share losses in this way, no loss becomes a burden for any particular member of the group.

Which of the following best states the principle of insurance we have just covered?

A. Many share the losses of a few.

B. Few share the losses of many.

Answer: A is correct.

8. How does insurance help many people share losses? Let's look at a simplified example.

   In the imaginary town of Middlefield there are 200 homes. Each home is worth $100,000.

   If a fire destroyed all the homes in Middlefield at one time, what would be the total dollar loss? $_____

   Answer: $20 million

9. Twenty million dollars! That's a lot of money. Of course all those homes are not likely to burn at once. Let's say that in Middlefield, one house burns each year.
   A. What is the yearly cost of this loss? $_____
   B. If every Middlefield homeowner (all 200 families) shared equally in the loss of that one house, what would the individual contribution be? $_____

   Answer: A. $100,000; B. $500

10. In insurance terms, the price people pay for insurance is called the **premium**.

Transferring the Risk of Loss

The insured exchanges a premium in return for insurance protection.

People who buy insurance exchange a *certain* cost (the premium) for the *uncertainty* that a loss will occur and its amount. By paying the premium, they transfer the risk of loss to the insurance company.

A. What is the uncertainty of loss? _____

B. What is the certain cost of insurance called? _____

Answer: A. Whether a loss will occur, when it will occur (timing), what the amount of the loss will be; B. The premium

11. Using the following phrases, construct a definition of insurance.

    in exchange for a certain cost   _____
    by transferring the risk of loss   _____
    to the insurance company   _____
    many share the losses of a few   _____

Answer: Many share the losses of a few by transferring the risk of loss to the insurance company in exchange for a certain cost.

The Law of Large Numbers

12. So you won't get the wrong idea, we should point out here that most insurance companies would not agree to insure every house in only one town, such as Middlefield. Insurance companies prefer to insure large numbers of people over a broad area.

    Which of the following examples best illustrate that principle?

    A. Company A insures 1,000,000 families in 15 states.
    B. Company B insures 500 families in two small towns.
    C. Company C insures 500,000 families in six states.

Answer: A is the best example. C is another good example.

13. What is the reason for this? Let's say that according to past experience, one home out of 1,000 will have a fire each year. Now suppose there is a community that has exactly 1,000 homes. If, at the end of one year, no home in that community had burned, would it mean that the statistic was wrong? No. The statistic was not developed based on experience with only 1,000 homes in one community. It was developed using millions of homes over wide areas of the country.

To check the validity of the statistic, you would have to look at not just 1,000 homes but (2,000/10,000/millions of) _____ homes.

Answer: millions of

14. The principle of obtaining enough examples to develop or confirm a given statistic is called the **law of large numbers**.

The Law of Large Numbers

> **THE LARGER THE SAMPLE, THE MORE ACCURATE THE PREDICTION**

Insurance companies use the law of large numbers to predict their losses. This means that a company can do which of the following?
A. Identify exactly which individuals in a group will have an accident
B. Predict about how many accidents will happen
C. Predict the approximate cost of the accidents
D. Determine exactly when each accident will occur

Answer: B and C are correct.

15. Suppose an insurance company insured every home in just one small town. It has charged a premium based upon statistics developed using millions of homes over wide areas of the country. Select the correct statement.
A. The losses in the town will probably not be the same as the statistic, and the company's actual loss experience will be somewhat different from what it expected.
B. The losses in the town probably will be the same as the statistic, and the company's actual loss experience will be almost exactly as expected.

Answer: A is correct.

16. The company, of course, will want to be able to predict its loss experience with a high degree of accuracy. What, then, must it do? _____

Answer: Insure many homes over a wide area of the country.

17. Closely related to the law of large numbers is another principle referred to as **spread of risk**. In addition to insuring large numbers of homes or other property, a company will want to insure property that represents different probabilities of loss. For example, the Florida coast is exposed to the risk of property damage that arises from hurricanes. Although hurricanes are not very frequent, they can cause a lot of damage when they do occur.

How could a company afford to insure homes along the Florida coast against property damage? _____

Answer: By not insuring every home along the Florida coast and by also insuring a large number of homes further inland and in other areas of the country.

Elements of Insurability

18. Not every risk is insurable. A risk must usually meet certain requirements in order to be insurable.

Insurability Rule #1: Large Numbers of Insureds

There must be a lot of people sharing risk of loss in order for the law of large numbers to work.

The first requirement is that there must be a *large number of persons available for insurance who have a similar potential for loss.* The law of large numbers works only when there are sufficient numbers of potential insureds who have a similar chance for loss to make the chances of loss predictable.

A. Suppose that millions of families in the country desired to obtain insurance against the possibility that fire might destroy their homes. Are there sufficient numbers of people involved to make this an insurable risk?   ( ) Yes   ( ) No

B. Suppose that all of the bullfighters in the United States desired insurance to protect them against the losses of being gored by a bull. Are there sufficient numbers of people involved to make this an insurable risk?   ( ) Yes   ( ) No

Answer: A. Yes; B. No

19. The second requirement is that if a loss occurs, it must be a *definite (or real) loss* and *the loss should be difficult, if not impossible, to counterfeit.*

Insurability Rule #2: No Counterfeits

A loss must be real and difficult to counterfeit.

Death is probably the best example of a definite loss, but there are many insurable risks that do not deal with something as clear cut as an individual's death. For example, you can buy insurance to cover theft losses even though it can be hard to determine in some cases whether property was stolen or simply misplaced.

Imagine that all motorists wanted insurance to pay for damages should the windshields in their automobiles be broken.

A. Are there sufficient numbers of people to make this an insurable risk?   ( ) Yes   ( ) No

B. If a loss occurs, is it definite?   ( ) Yes   ( ) No

Answer: A. Yes; B. Yes (and of course such insurance protection is available).

20. The third requirement is that a loss must be *accidental* in nature. This means that it must generally be unexpected and beyond the insured's control.

Insurability Rule #3: Accidental Loss

A loss must not be intentional.

Suppose that every person in the country who owns a red car wants insurance to pay for a new paint job because of red paint inevitably fading over a period of years. There are sufficient numbers of people involved to make this an insurable risk, and there is a definite loss, but since the loss is not accidental, it would not be insurable.

Suppose people wanted insurance to have a new paint job done on their automobile if a vandal scraped the car all over with a nail.

A. Is such a loss accidental (from the insured's point of view)?
( ) Yes ( ) No

B. Is this loss insurable? ( ) Yes ( ) No

Answer: A. Yes; B. Yes

21. The fourth requirement is that the loss must be *large enough to create a financial burden for the individual involved.*

Insurability Rule #4: Financial Burden

A loss must be hard to bear.

Suppose that parents across the country desire insurance coverage to reimburse them for the cost of replacing the pens and pencils their children lose in school each year.

A. Are there enough persons involved to make the risk insurable?
   ( ) Yes   ( ) No
B. Is there a definite loss?   ( ) Yes   ( ) No
C. Is the loss accidental?   ( ) Yes   ( ) No
D. Is the loss large enough to create a financial burden?   ( ) Yes   ( ) No

Answer: A. Yes; B. Yes; C. Yes; D. No (it would probably cost more to administer the insurance program than it would to simply buy new pens and pencils).

22. Suppose all automobile owners desired insurance protection to reimburse them in case their cars were stolen. Using the requirements we've discussed so far, is this risk insurable? ( ) Yes ( ) No

Why or why not? _____
_____
_____

Answer: Yes. There are sufficient numbers, a definite loss which is accidental from the insured's standpoint, and the loss is large enough to create a financial burden.

23. The fifth requirement for a risk to be insurable is that the insurance must be *affordable*. This requirement does not relate to the insured's budget, but rather to the value of the item insured—it means that the cost of the insurance should generally be a small fraction of that item's value.

Insurability Rule #5: Must Be Affordable

The cost of insurance must generally be relatively small compared to the value of the item insured.

Suppose a man wants to buy insurance on an old barn that's valued at $2,000. The premium for this coverage is $1,500 a year. Is this insurance a wise buy for the man?   ( ) Yes   ( ) No
Why or why not? _____
_____
_____

Answer: No. The certain cost of the insurance (the premium) is almost as much as the value of the property, the loss of which is uncertain. There is little transfer of risk in this situation.

24. A sixth requirement is that the cost of the loss must be *calculable*. This means that there must be some way of expressing the loss in monetary terms. In many cases, this is a fairly straightforward procedure.

Insurability Rule #6: Must Be Calculable

The loss must be expressed as a monetary amount.

If a collision crushes a car's fender, how is the cost of the loss determined?
_____
_____
_____

Answer: It is the cost to repair or replace the fender.

25. You may have heard the expression "pain and suffering" used in connection with settling lawsuits. Although it may seem impossible to measure pain and suffering in monetary terms, methods have been developed for arriving at dollar amounts that represent the value of the loss in such cases.

    As with pain and suffering, it is also impossible to reduce the value of a human life to a dollar amount. However, do you think it may be possible to make the financial loss that results upon the death of an individual calculable for purposes of insurance?   ( ) Yes   ( ) No

    Answer: Yes (if it were not possible, life insurance would not exist).

Insurability Rule #7: No Catastrophes

The loss must not be so large that it would bankrupt a company.

26. The seventh requirement is that the loss must *not routinely happen to a large number of insureds at the same time*. "Catastrophic" losses could bankrupt an insurance company. Remember the earlier example of a single company insuring all of the homes along the Florida coast? Explain the possibility for a catastrophic loss here. _____
_____
_____
_____

Answer: A hurricane could destroy all the homes at once, and the company would lose millions of dollars in a short time. All the homes can be insured, but by a number of different companies.

27. Finally, the risk to be insured must be a "pure risk" as opposed to a "speculative risk." Let's distinguish these terms.

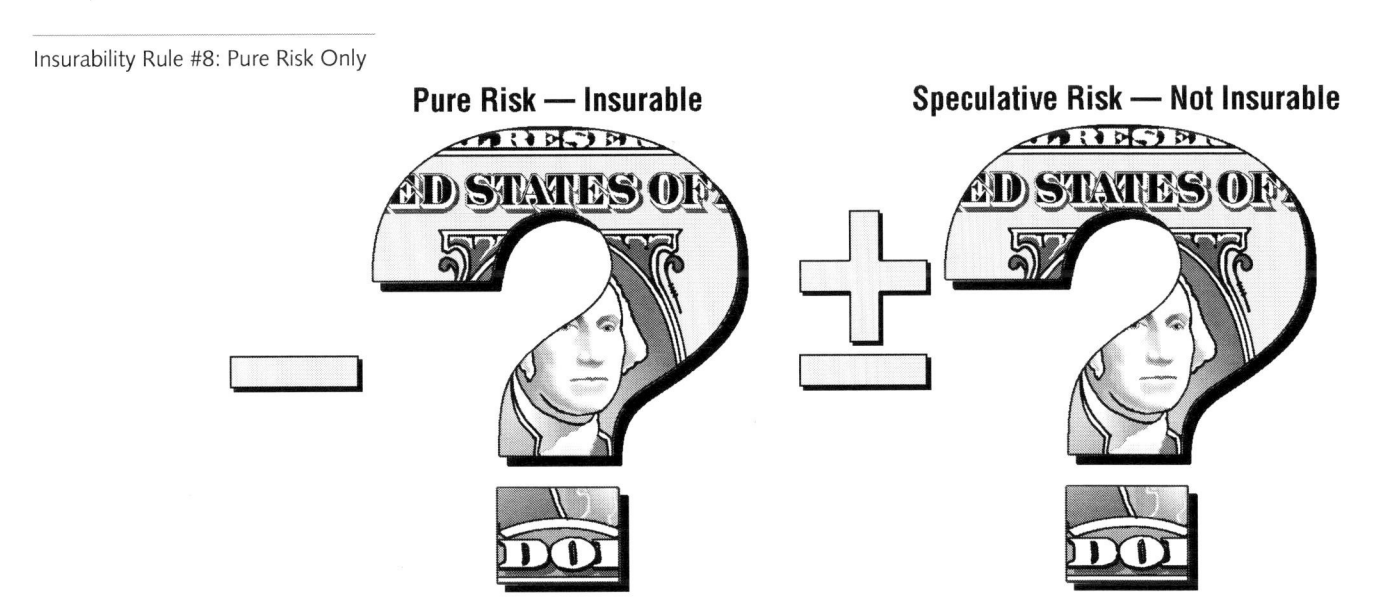

Insurability Rule #8: Pure Risk Only

Pure Risk — Insurable   **Speculative Risk — Not Insurable**

A "pure" risk does not include the possibility of gain

A **speculative risk** is one that involves the possibility of either loss or gain, such as gambling. Gamblers place their bets knowing they may lose their money but hoping to get back more than they have risked.

A **pure risk** involves the possibility of loss only. If you own a car, it may be damaged in a collision or it may not be. A collision will cause you a financial loss, but the lack of a collision will not result in any gain to you.

Speculative risks are *not* insurable because they are generally *created* by the person involved. There is no speculative risk for gamblers until they place a bet. However, the risk of collision is inherent in owning a car. We don't create a risk by buying a car. The risk of financial loss due to collision exists for anyone who owns a car.

A. Carl takes a financial risk by investing $10,000 in stocks. This is an example of a (speculative/pure) _____ risk.
B. Is the risk Carl is taking insurable or uninsurable? _____
C. Joanna purchases a diamond necklace for $10,000, taking the risk that it may be lost or stolen. This is an example of a (speculative/pure) _____ risk.
D. Is the risk we've described in regard to Joanna's diamond necklace insurable or uninsurable? _____

Answer: A. speculative; B. uninsurable; C. pure; D. insurable

Insurable Interest

28. A basic principle of insurance states that in order to benefit from insurance you must face the possibility of financial loss in regard to the subject insured. This financial interest in the subject of insurance is referred to as an **insurable interest**.

Principle of Insurable Interest

A relationship or condition that loss or destruction of life or property would cause a financial loss.

In the case of property insurance, the insurable interest must exist at the time of loss. In the case of life insurance, the insurable interest must exist at the time the policy is purchased.

A. In which of the following property would you have an insurable interest?
   1. Your own home
   2. Your neighbor's home
   3. The Empire State Building
   4. Your own car

B. Let's assume you don't have an insurable interest in the Brooklyn Bridge (you wouldn't fall for that old swindle, would you?). Therefore, it (would/would not) _____ be possible for you to buy insurance on that property.

Answer: A. 1 and 4 are correct; B. would not

29. Donald thinks the house his neighbor owns is a fire trap. Donald thinks he could make money by purchasing insurance on his neighbor's house because, if the house actually did catch fire, Donald could probably collect more in benefits than he paid in premiums. What's wrong with Donald's scheme?

_____
_____

Answer: Donald can't purchase insurance on his neighbor's house because he does not have an insurable interest in it.

30. Joe buys a $100,000 home using $20,000 of his own money and $80,000 borrowed from the ABC Mortgage Company. Who has an insurable interest in Joe's new home? Remember, we defined insurable interest as the chance of a financial loss regarding the subject of insurance.
    A. Joe
    B. The ABC Mortgage Company

Answer: Both A and B are correct.

31. When two or more parties stand to lose financially should a loss occur, this is known as a **joint insurable interest**.

    The situation with regard to Joe's new home is a case of
    A. insurable interest.
    B. joint insurable interest.

Answer: B is correct.

Indemnification

32. After a covered loss occurs, the company must determine exactly how much the insured should be paid. Under the principle of **indemnity**, a person is restored to the approximate financial position he or she was in before the loss occurred. When someone is paid for a loss, it is said that he or she is **indemnified** for the loss.

Principle of Indemnity

The insured should be paid no more and no less than the cost of a loss.

A. Which of the following are examples of indemnification *by an insurance company*?
   1. John's house burns down after being struck by lightning. John's insurance company pays the full cost of having it rebuilt.
   2. Someone steals Susan's fur coat, valued at $7,000. She reports the loss and receives a check from her insurance company for $7,000.
   3. In retaliation for an insult, Peter breaks all the windows out of his neighbor's car. A court determines that Peter must pay his neighbor $3,000 for the damage. Since the act was deliberate, no insurance coverage applies to Peter's obligation to pay.

B. An insured bought an automobile for $20,000. After two years, the car was worth $15,000. If an accident then demolished it, what would be the amount of the financial loss suffered by the insured? $ _____

Answer: A. 1 and 2 are correct (Peter will indemnify his neighbor for the glass breakage, but the insurance company will not pay); B. $15,000

33. Irene bought a new car four years ago for $25,000. It's worth $17,000 today. A collision destroyed it yesterday.
    A. Using the principle of indemnity, which of the following is the amount she should receive for her loss?
        1. $25,000
        2. $500
        3. $17,000
    B. Why would Irene not get $25,000? _____
    _____
    C. Why wouldn't Irene get $500? _____
    _____
    D. Irene would receive $17,000 because that amount restores her to the approximate financial condition she was in before the loss occurred. This is a specific example of the principle of _____.

    Answer: A. 3 is correct; B. The car is not worth as much now as when it was new; C. The car is worth more than $500; D. indemnity

34. There are exceptions to the principle of indemnity. For example, suppose John Davis is cut on the face in an auto accident caused by Linda Kates. Even after cosmetic surgery, he is left with visible scars. Let's say that John's medical bills total $5,000—that's the amount of his financial loss. But knowing that a court could award something to John for his disfigurement, Linda's liability insurer might offer John more than $5,000 to settle the claim.

    Another exception to the principle of indemnity occurs when a court awards **punitive damages.** Punitive damages are not designed to compensate an injured party for a financial loss but are intended to punish a wrongdoer. They are awarded when an injury is caused intentionally or out of recklessness.

    George Adler's trash fire got out of control and did $1,000 of damage to Ellen Lee's garage. A jury finds that George acted recklessly when he left the fire unattended and awards Ellen $5,000. The first $1,000 of the award is intended to indemnify Ellen for her repair bills. The other $4,000 of the award is _____.

    Answer: punitive damages

We have now acquainted you with some of the fundamental concepts of insurance. Familiarity with the concepts presented in this unit is essential to understanding what insurance is and how it works. In the next unit, we will take a broad look at the insurance industry as a whole. We will look at the types of companies that employ these concepts as part of their daily business, and we will look at how the government regulates those companies.

UNIT 3

An Overview of the Insurance Industry

1. In this unit, we will look at the structure of the insurance industry and the methods the government uses to regulate it. This unit will describe:

    ■ the four major branches of insurance,

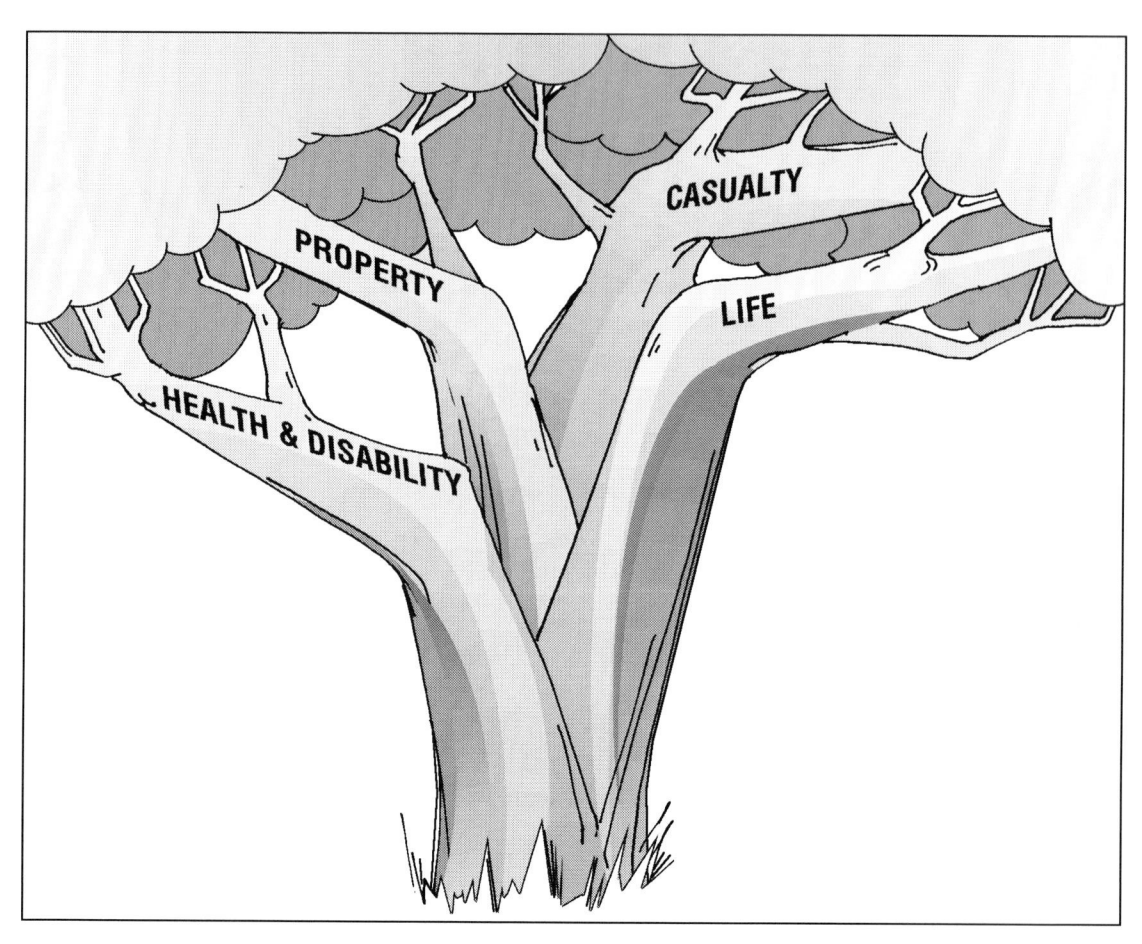

    ■ the major types of insurance companies, and

    ■ the areas of insurance company operation that the government regulates.

    After learning these things, you will be ready for our next unit's more detailed discussion of the work done by various individuals in the insurance industry.

MAJOR BRANCHES OF INSURANCE

2. There are four major branches, or "lines," of insurance, each of which was developed to handle a broad category of risks.

The Four Major Branches of Insurance

Life insurance is designed to handle the risks of dying too soon and leaving a surviving family in financial difficulty or of living too long and not having enough money in retirement.

Health and disability insurance are designed to handle the risks of incurring medical expenses or not being able to earn a living after getting sick or injured.

In this course, we will not deal with these branches of insurance, but you should be aware that your company, your agency, and perhaps even you someday may work with coverages that come under these categories.

Ask your supervisor if your company writes or is affiliated with a company that writes life or health and disability insurance.

Indicate which branch of insurance is designed to handle each of the following categories of risk by placing an "L" for life insurance or an "H/D" for health and disability insurance in the blank before each item.

    __L__ A. Outliving one's financial resources

    __L__ B. Losses created by an individual's death

    __H/D__ C. Loss of income due to injury or sickness

    __H/D__ D. Cost of medical care

Answer: L A.; L B.; H/D C.; H/D D.

Property Insurance

3. The remaining two branches of insurance make up the property-casualty insurance industry.

    Property insurance is relatively simple to define. It includes many types of insurance designed to cover property losses—the risks that we will suffer financial losses because things we own are damaged or destroyed.

    There are three basic types of property loss:

    1. Loss of the article itself
    2. Loss of income from the use of the article
    3. The extra expense incurred due to the loss of the article

    Indicate whether the following property losses are type 1, 2, or 3.

        __2__ A. A hotel burns to the ground. In the year required to rebuild, the hotel loses over $2 million in room rentals.

        __3__ B. A large automobile agency warehouse burns. Its owners rent office space from a local motel until the damage has been repaired.

        __1__ C. One morning, a homeowner discovers that a valuable painting is missing.

        __3__ D. A large fire destroys a city newspaper building. To continue publishing, its owners rent another press at one-third additional cost.

4. Some types of insurance generally considered to be property insurance include the following:

    - Dwelling insurance
    - Homeowners
    - Commercial property insurance
    - Inland marine
    - Ocean marine

    Later we'll look more closely at each of these types of insurance.

Casualty Insurance

5. **Casualty insurance** is more difficult to define because it includes a wide variety of basically unrelated insurance products.

    One of the most important types of casualty insurance is **liability insurance**. **Liability losses** are losses that occur as a result of the insured's interactions with others or their property. Probably the best example of this would be an auto accident. Let's say Arthur is backing out of his driveway and hits Beatrice's parked car. Result: $600 damage. Because Arthur was at fault, he is legally responsible, or liable, for those damages, and he must pay to have Beatrice's car repaired. Liability insurance would protect Arthur from having to pay for those damages out of his own pocket.

    Select the examples of liability losses.

    A. When a truck hits a school bus, 15 children are sent to the hospital with serious injuries. The truck driver was at fault.
    B. Tornado-like winds damage a very expensive home.
    C. A toy with steel-tipped arrows accidentally causes three children injury during a neighborhood game. The toy manufacturer was at fault because the toy has a dangerous design.
    D. An auto owner accidentally sets his car on fire when he drops a cigarette onto the seat. The fire destroys the car.

    Answer: A and C are correct. Item D is not a liability loss, since it does not involve the property of someone other than the owner.

6. To be legally liable, the individual must generally be guilty of **negligence**—the failure to use proper care in personal actions. If negligence results in harm to another, the individual is liable for the resulting damages.

Elaine has a swimming pool in her backyard. No fence is around the yard or the pool. Unfortunately, one evening a neighbor's child falls into the pool and nearly drowns.

A. Could Elaine be found negligent for failing to fence in her swimming pool? (✓) Yes ( ) No

B. Might Elaine be held liable for this child's injuries? (✓) Yes ( ) No

Answer: A. Yes; B. Yes

7. People in the insurance industry often call liability losses **third-party losses**.

The Three Parties in a Liability Loss

FIRST PARTY   **SECOND PARTY**   **THIRD PARTY**

Liability coverage benefits are paid to an injured third party.

The insured is the first party. The insurance company is the second party. The person to whom the insured is liable for damages is the _____ party.

Answer: third

8. Just as you can purchase property insurance to protect you from financial loss should your property be damaged, you can purchase liability insurance to protect you from financial loss should you become legally liable for injury to another or damage to another's property.

   Identify which of the following losses could be covered by property insurance and which by liability insurance by putting a "P" for property insurance or an "L" for liability insurance in the blank before each item.

   ____ A. Your valuable diamond ring is missing from your safe.
   ____ B. You cause damage to another individual's car.
   ____ C. Your child injures another child.
   ____ D. You lose your entire house and its contents to fire.

Answer: P A.; L B.; L C.; P D.

9. Although insurance for liability risks is an important casualty coverage, there are many other types of insurance that have traditionally been considered casualty insurance. Casualty insurance can also include the following types of insurance:

   - Aviation
   - Auto
   - Boiler and machinery
   - Crime
   - Workers' compensation
   - Surety bonds

   Later we'll look more closely at each of these types of casualty insurance.

   A. In general, property insurance protects against _____.

   B. One of the more important risks covered by casualty insurance is liability risk, which insures against _____.

Answer: A. loss to property; B. legal liability for damage to someone or to his or her property

TYPES OF INSURANCE COMPANIES

10. There are basically five types of property-casualty insurance companies, corresponding to the five ways in which companies raise the money necessary to begin business and choose to enroll their customers for insurance.

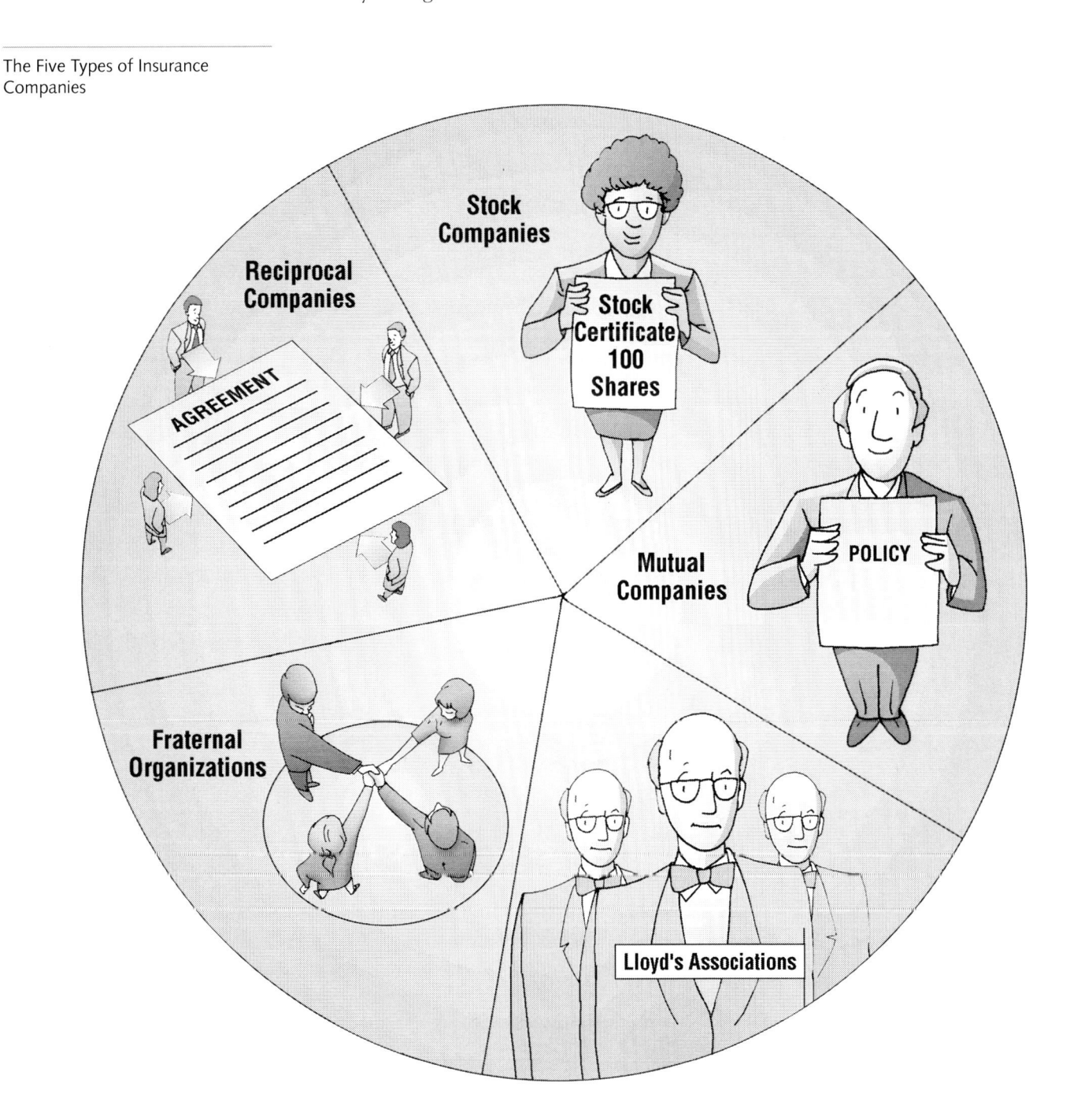

The Five Types of Insurance Companies

Stock Companies

11. People sometimes refer to **stock companies** as *capital-stock* companies. When this type of company is formed, it is incorporated and sells stock to raise the capital it needs to start doing business. The people who purchase the stock are the stockholders, and they own the company.

Stock Company

A stock company is owned by its stockholders.

If the business is profitable, the stockholders may receive dividends. In a stock company, dividends are generally *not* paid to the policyholders, who are the company's customers. Although it may be possible for stockholders to purchase policies from the company or for policyholders to purchase stock, in a stock insurance company the owners and the customers are generally two separate parties, as with most corporate businesses.

Which of the following is a description of a stock insurance company?

A. Last year, losses at ABC Insurance Company were high, so it paid only a small dividend to its stockholders.
B. DEF Insurance Company experienced record profits and as a result raised the dividend it paid to policyholders.
C. UEW Insurance Company paid a modest dividend to policyholders after an unremarkable year.

Answer: A is correct.

Mutual Companies

12. A **mutual company** functions differently from a stock company. A mutual company does not sell stock or have stockholders. The owners are the policyholders themselves. As owners, policyholders can vote to elect company managers. Policyholders also share in the company's operating results either by receiving a dividend or by a reduced premium.

Unit 3 An Overview of the Insurance Industry   43

Mutual Company

A mutual company is owned by its policyholders.

Write the word "stock" or "mutual," as appropriate, after each of the following descriptions.
A. King County Insurance Company has policyholders in all 50 states. The annual dividend paid to them helps reduce their out-of-pocket costs for insurance coverage. _____
B. Dove Insurance Company declares a two-for-one stock split. _____
C. The dividend for each policyholder of Hunters Insurance Company amounts to $20 per year. _____
D. Each year the policyholders of the Steady Insurance Company elect a governing board to manage the company's operations. _____

Answer: A. mutual; B. stock; C. mutual; D. mutual

Other Types of Insurers

13. The third form of company organization, **reciprocal companies**, are not as common as stock and mutual companies. The word "reciprocate" means to give and take—so a member of a reciprocal company (sometimes referred to as a *reciprocal*, for short) agrees to share the risk of loss with all the other members. In a sense, all "members" insure each other and share their losses with each other. As with a mutual company, the reciprocal members vote for and control company management.

Reciprocal Company

A reciprocal company is a group of people who agree to share each other's losses.

For each of the following, determine whether the description fits a stock, mutual, or reciprocal company by writing the correct word after the description.

A. Oak Tree Insurance Company is having an annual election to determine its Board of Directors. Each stockholder will vote in proportion to the numbers of shares of stock he or she owns. _____

B. All the members of Firehouse of America Insurance Company each paid $400 this year to indemnify those members who suffered losses during the year. _____

C. The policyholders of Uppercrust Insurance Company each can cast a vote to determine whom the company's management team will be _____.

Answer: A. stock; B. reciprocal; C. mutual

14. A fourth type of **insuring organization** is a **Lloyd's association**. You may have heard of the famous group called "Lloyd's of London." Lloyd's is not actually a company, but a syndicate of private individuals or groups of individuals who voluntarily agree to issue insurance. Insurers that are similarly organized are also referred to as Lloyd's associations, even though they aren't affiliated with Lloyd's of London.

A fifth type of insurer is a **fraternal organization**. A fraternal organization is a society or order organized solely for the benefit of its members and their beneficiaries, not for profit. Fraternals offer insurance only to their members.

Lloyd's Association

A Lloyd's association is a group of insurers who voluntarily agree to provide coverage.

Fraternal Organization

A fraternal organization is a society or order that offers insurance only to its members.

Identify each of the following types of insuring organizations by writing an "S" for stock, an "M" for mutual, an "R" for reciprocal, an "L" for Lloyd's or an "F" for fraternal in the blank prior to the appropriate description.

____ A. The policyholders of this type of company receive dividends and vote for the management of the company.

____ B. This type of insuring organization is actually a syndicate of private insurers.

____ C. This company raises capital by selling stock and distributes dividends to stockholders, not policyholders.

____ D. The members of this company agree to share each other's losses.

____ E. This organization is a society or order that offers insurance only to its members.

Answer: M A.; L B.; S C.; R D.; F E.

Ask your supervisor what type of company (or companies) you are affiliated with: stock, mutual, reciprocal, or Lloyd's association.

INSURANCE REGULATION

State and Federal Roles

15. From its beginnings, the individual states have regulated insurance industry activities within their respective borders. Current law generally permits the federal government to intervene only when state regulation proves to be inadequate. This gives the various state governments an incentive to make sure they do a good job. While the federal government can influence these activities, it is generally up to the states to enact and enforce the laws that regulate the insurance business.

Regulation by the States

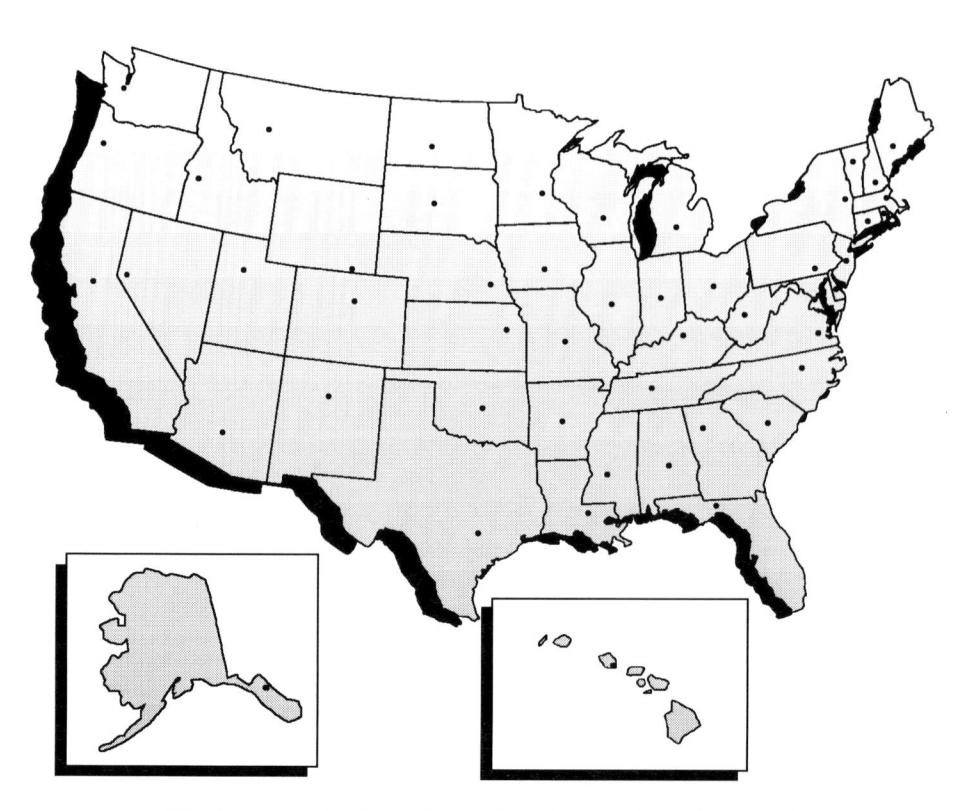

The insurance business is regulated primarily at the state level.

Each state legislature is responsible for enacting the state's insurance laws, and the insurance department of each state administers them. The head of the insurance department is known as the Insurance Commissioner, although this individual is referred to as the Director or Superintendent of Insurance in some states.

In the U.S., the insurance business is subject to regulation by
A. the Federal Trade Commission.
B. the President of the United States.
C. the U.S. Senate and House of Representatives.
D. each state's Insurance Commissioner.

Answer: D is correct.

Company Authorization

Admitted/Nonadmitted

16. One of the ways states regulate the insurance business is by deciding which insurance companies (often simply called "insurers") are authorized to conduct business within their borders. If an insurance company meets the state's requirements, the insurance department issues it a **certificate of authority**, and it becomes an **authorized insurer**, also known as an **admitted insurer**.

Ask your supervisor about the states in which your company is authorized to do business.

The XYZ Insurance Company receives a certificate of authority to operate in Texas. In Texas, then, XYZ Insurance Company is an _____ insurer.

Answer: authorized or admitted (either answer is correct)

17. A company that does not have a certificate of authority to operate in a given state is known as an **unauthorized**, or **nonadmitted insurer** in that state.

The XYZ Insurance Company has a certificate of authority only from Texas and Oklahoma.
A. In Oklahoma, XYZ Insurance Company is a/an _____ _____ insurer.
B. In New Mexico, XYZ Insurance Company is a/an _____ _____ insurer.

Answer: A. authorized or admitted; B. unauthorized or nonadmitted

Domestic/Foreign/Alien

18. In its home state, or **state of domicile**, a company is known as a **domestic company**. If it is admitted to other states, it operates in those states as a **foreign company**.

Domestic or Foreign?

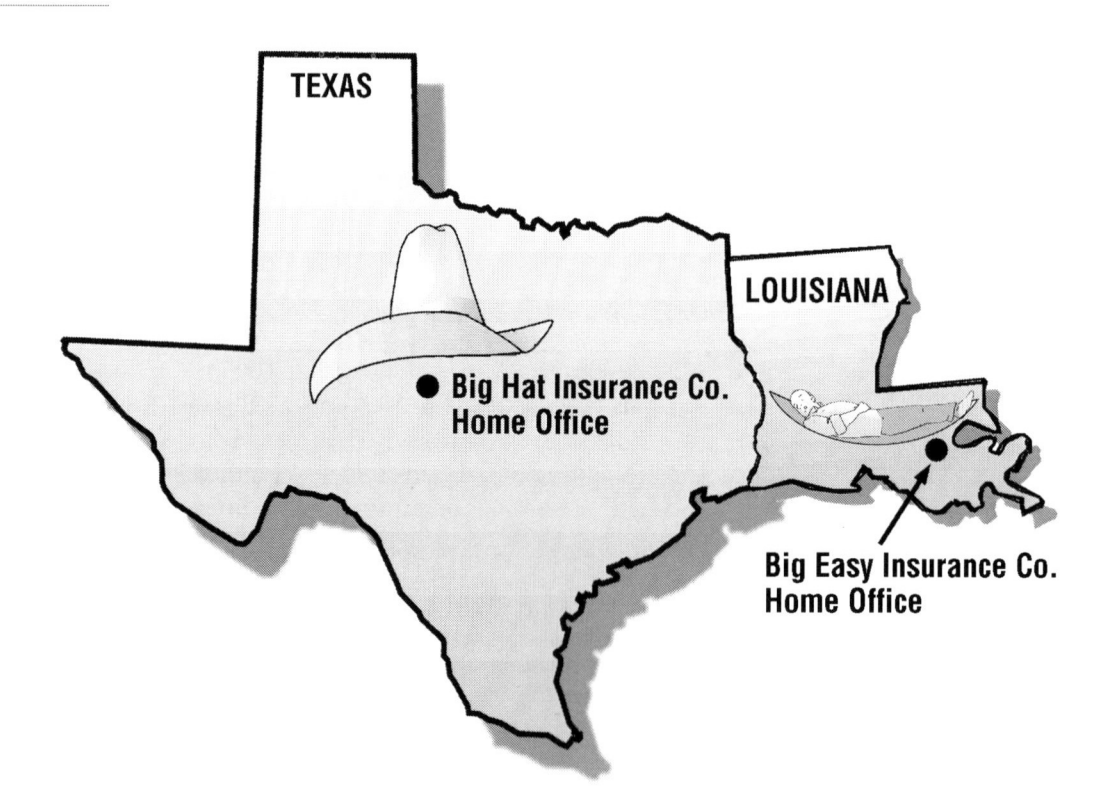

The Big Hat Insurance Company is domiciled in Texas. The Big Easy Insurance Company is domiciled in Louisiana. Both companies are authorized to do business in both Texas and Louisiana.

A. In Texas, the Big Hat Insurance Company is a (domestic/foreign) _____ company.

B. In Louisiana, the Big Hat Insurance Company is a (domestic/foreign) _____ company.

C. In Texas, the Big Easy Insurance Company is a (domestic/foreign) _____ company.

D. In Louisiana, the Big Easy Insurance Company is a (domestic/foreign) _____ company.

Answer: A. domestic; B. foreign; C. foreign; D. domestic

19. You may be wondering, if "foreign" means "out-of-state," then what do we call a company from another country? If a company that is domiciled in a different country is admitted to do business in a state, it is known as an **alien insurer** in that state.

    The Guday Insurance Company is domiciled in Australia. In any U.S. state in which it was admitted to do business, it would be known as a/an (foreign/alien) _____ insurer.

    Answer: alien

Financial Regulation

20. One of the most important aspects of insurance regulation is helping to ensure that insurers remain solvent—that is, financially healthy. The methods insurance departments use to accomplish this include the following:

    - Companies must have specified minimum amounts of capital and/or surplus to begin and continue operations in a state.

    - Companies must submit annual reports on their financial condition to the insurance commissioners of the states in which they do business.

    - Every three to five years, insurance departments conduct regular onsite field examinations of companies. They can also order special investigations of insurers as necessary.

    - All companies must use the same set of standard accounting procedures.

    - Companies must set aside a portion of every premium they collect as a reserve against future claims.

    - The law generally limits the types of investments that insurers may make with their funds to those that are relatively conservative, such as bonds and mortgages.

Financial Examination

Insurance departments help ensure that companies stay financially healthy.

The goal of capital and/or surplus requirements, annual reports, examinations, and other financial regulation is to help ensure that insurers remain (profitable/solvent/incorporated) _____ .

Answer: solvent

Rate Regulation

21. Insurance departments may also regulate an insurer's rates—the amounts they charge the public for insurance. One purpose of rate regulation is to help ensure that insurers stay solvent: rates must be high enough to cover

an insurer's expected losses and expenses. Other purposes include making sure that insurers don't make rates too high compared to the value that consumers receive and ensuring that rates don't unfairly discriminate against certain people or groups.

The methods insurance departments use to regulate rates vary from state to state and by line of insurance. In some cases, where plenty of insurers are competing for a particular line of business, the insurance department may allow competition among the insurers to establish the level of rates. In other cases, companies may have to file their rates and have them approved by the insurance department before they may use them. For some coverages, certain states determine what rates companies must use.

There are variations in between: for example, insurance departments may require companies to file their rates for particular lines of business but may allow companies to use those rates without waiting for the department's approval. But even where rates are set by competition among companies, the insurance department may ask companies to justify the rates they are using and may disapprove any rates that are inadequate (too low) or excessive (too high) or that discriminate unfairly because they are based on something other than risk-related characteristics.

JOB BUILDER

Ask your supervisor how the insurance department regulates the rates for various lines of insurance in your state.

A. The ABC Insurance Company wants to price its policy very low in order to sell more policies than its competitors. However, its proposed rates are so low the company may not be able to pay its claims. The insurance department would likely disapprove these rates on the basis that they were (inadequate/excessive/unfairly discriminatory) ___inadequate___

B. Since no other company writes the line of business that DEF Insurance Company specializes in, it could charge just about any amount it wanted for its policies. However, the insurance department could disapprove too high a rate on the basis that it was (inadequate/excessive/unfairly discriminatory) ___excessive___

C. Tim and Tom are the same age, have similar kinds of cars, and similar driving records. Suppose GHI Insurance Company were to charge Tim more for his car insurance than it charges Tom because Tim isn't very sophisticated about insurance and won't realize the company is taking advantage of him. The insurance department would disapprove GHI's rate to Tim on the basis that it was (inadequate/excessive/unfairly discriminatory) ___unfairly discriminatory___.

Answer: A. inadequate; B. excessive; C. unfairly discriminatory

Regulation of Policy Forms

22. Although insurance is not a simple product, insurance regulators have taken a number of approaches to keep it from becoming overly complex.

    - **Standard Policies.** For certain types of coverage, the law may prescribe the wording of the entire policy.

    - **Mandatory Provisions.** In some cases, the law may prescribe only the wording of certain provisions that must be included in certain types of policies.

    - **Policy Filing.** The law may require companies to file certain types of policies with the insurance department and receive its approval before using them.

    - **Easy-to-Read Policies.** Regulators may require that insurers write their policies using simplified wording, make certain provisions appear separately from other copy, and use at least a certain size or style of type.

    While such requirements limit the variety and flexibility of coverages available to consumers, they also help make policies easier for people to understand and to compare.

    We've now covered four aspects of the insurance business that insurance departments regulate. Can you name them?

    A. *company authorizations*
    B. *Financial regulations*
    C. *Rate regulation*
    D. *Regulation of policy forms*

    Answer: In any order: A. Company authorization; B. Financial regulation; C. Rate regulation; D. Regulation of policy forms

Licensing of Personnel

23. Insurance departments also regulate the insurance business by requiring people in certain positions to be licensed. By establishing licensing requirements—such as that an individual be of a certain age, have no history of criminal wrongdoing and pass a qualification exam—insurance departments help assure that persons in those positions are of good character and possess a minimum level of competence.

License Required

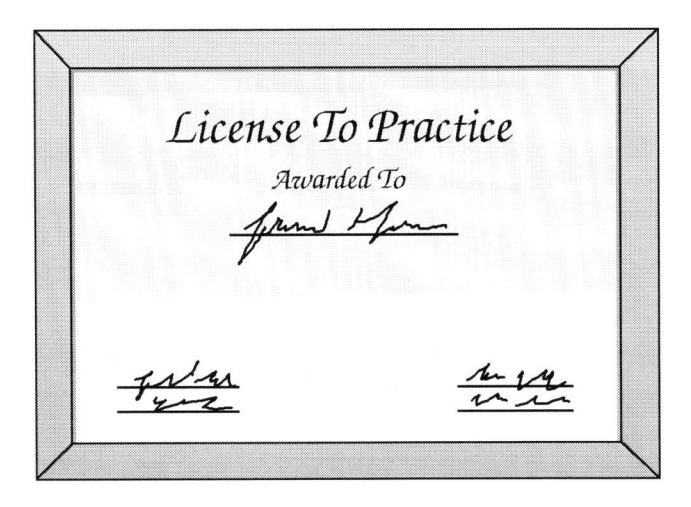

To obtain and keep their licenses, insurance practitioners must be competent and trustworthy.

All states require those who represent insurance companies in sales situations with consumers to be licensed as **agents, brokers,** or **producers**. Some states also require claims representatives to be licensed as **adjusters**. In the next unit, we'll talk in more detail about these people and others who are involved in the insurance process.

John Kay wishes to become an agent. In order to ensure that John is of sufficiently good character and possesses the knowledge required to do his job properly for the public, the insurance department will require John to obtain an agent's license .

Answer: license

Trade Practices

24. The insurance department also regulates the manner in which companies and their representatives conduct themselves in dealings with the public. Certain practices are prohibited by law. For example, agents and brokers must avoid any type of deceptive sales practice, particularly any **misrepresentation** of policy features, terms, or benefits. There is also a list of unfair claim settlement practices that adjusters must avoid.

    The goal of trade practice regulation is to establish minimum standards of fair dealing with the public. Those who violate these rules are subject to penalties ranging from censure, to fines, to loss of their licenses. The companies they represent may also incur fines and other sanctions if they were negligent in supervising those individuals' activities.

    In order to make a sale, agent Solow assures a consumer that a policy includes a coverage that the company does not offer. Which of the following statements is correct?

    A. Agent Solow is guilty of misrepresentation.
    B. Agent Solow could lose his insurance license.
    C. Agent Solow has not broken any trade practice law.

THE GOVERNMENT AS AN INSURER

25. In some cases, the federal or the state government becomes involved in the insurance business not as a regulator but as an insurer. This is done when the public needs some type of coverage that the private insurance industry cannot provide, or cannot provide as effectively, as the government.

    The federal government operates several property-casualty insurance programs. Probably the most well known are the National Flood Insurance Program, which makes flood insurance available to property owners, and the Federal Crop Insurance Program, which offers farmers protection against crop damage from drought, insects, hail, and other perils. Some private insurers aid the government by providing coverage under these programs or helping to administer them.

    Many state governments are active in **workers' compensation**. In some states, the law requires employers to buy their workers' compensation coverage from the state. In some others, employers can buy coverage from either the state program or private insurers.

Ask your supervisor if your company writes workers' compensation coverage and, if so, whether your state allows employers to buy this coverage from private insurers.

Fill in the blank with the correct response.

A. Primarily, the role of the government in relation to the insurance industry is that of (regulator/insurer) _____.

B. However, in some cases the government also becomes involved in the insurance industry as a/an (regulator/insurer) _____.

Answer: A. regulator; B. insurer

We have given you a broad overview of the insurance industry and the basic concepts of insurance. In the next unit, we will take a closer look at insurance company operations and the people who perform the many vital functions necessary for insurance to be offered and delivered to the public.

UNIT 4

The People Behind the Promise

1. When people buy insurance policies, they are buying promises from insurance companies to pay in the event they incur losses. To make those promises a reality takes the coordinated and dedicated effort of many people. In this unit, we'll look at who is behind the promises to policyholders. In the course of describing these individuals' responsibilities, we will outline the *insurance process*—the series of steps that make up the insurance transaction from the initial purchase proposal through the issue of a policy and, in the event of a loss, the settlement of a claim. Specifically, we will:

   - discuss the general duties of agents and the different types of agents;
   - explain the function of underwriters;
   - describe the rate-making and rating procedures;
   - look at the individuals responsible for issuing insurance policies;
   - describe the activities of claims personnel; and
   - explain the important functions carried out by persons in various support departments of an insurance company.

Standing Behind the Promise

By the end of this unit, you will have a sense of the essential roles that all who are part of the insurance process play in offering and delivering the promise of financial stability to the public.

MARKETING

2. To begin the insurance process, insurance companies must have some way of contacting prospective clients. Some insurance companies sell directly to the public. They advertise their policies in bulk mailings or through advertisements on TV or some other media and then accept applications from people who respond by mail or phone. Insurers with this type of distribution system are known as **direct response** companies.

   Most insurance companies use salespeople—sometimes called producers—to market their products. Two types of producers are **agents** and **brokers**. Agents or brokers serve as a link between a company and a prospect or insured. They earn a commission on sales in return for their work. Most of the Marketing section of this unit deals with these salespeople.

   Which of the following examples describes the way a company that uses producers operates?

   A. Jay, a representative of ABC Insurance Company, discusses coverages with people who come to him for insurance. If they decide to buy, he accepts the premium from them and forwards it to ABC.

   B. Todd receives information about coverage available from XYZ Insurance Company in the mail. He fills out an application that was enclosed with the material and sends it back to XYZ.

   Answer: A is correct.

Types of Agents

3. Some agents have contracts to sell insurance for several insurance companies. These are known as **independent agents**.

   Some agents sell insurance for only one insurance company. They are known as **exclusive agents**. These are independent business people who have contracted to sell for the one company they represent. Another name for an exclusive agent is **captive agent**. There are also insurance companies known as **direct writers** whose sales representatives are actually employees of the company. These employees are paid a regular salary rather than earning a commission on sales as agents do. However, since these employees represent only one company, from a consumer's standpoint a direct writer looks very similar to a company that uses exclusive agents. In fact, sometimes the term "direct writer" is used to refer to companies that use exclusive agents as well as those that employ their sales representatives.

Ask your supervisor whether your company works with agents and, if so, whether they are independent agents or exclusive agents.

In the blank provided, identify the type of agent by writing "E" for exclusive or "I" for independent.

_____ A. Agent Phil Little represents ABC Insurance Company. As an employee of that company, he is paid a regular salary.

_____ B. Agent Ruth Horn represents the J&K Insurance Company, the L&M Insurance Company, and the P&Q Insurance Company. She decides which company will best suit the needs of a particular client, and each company pays her a commission on the business she places there.

_____ C. Agent Edgar Dodd represents only the XYZ Insurance Company. He earns a commission on each sale he makes.

Answer: E A.; I B.; E C.

Brokers

4. Another type of insurance salesperson is the **broker**. In practice, brokers operate much like independent agents in that they can negotiate with several different companies to place insurance business. However, brokers actually represent the insurance *purchaser* rather than the insurance company in those negotiations. Many companies use both brokers and agents in their distribution system.

   A. To obtain insurance for her multimillion dollar business, Georgette relies on the services of Arnold, who negotiates with several insurance companies on her behalf. Is Arnold an agent or a broker? _____

   B. To obtain insurance for his multinational business, Clint relies on the services of Dina, who will recommend that he purchase coverage from one of the several companies she represents. Is Dina an agent or a broker? _____

Answer: A. broker; B. agent

Sales and Related Activities

5. Agents and brokers are involved in a number of activities in their roles as sales representatives. Let's look first at selling insurance. There are a number of terms that relate to the selling process that you should know.

Sales Activities

Agents and brokers are responsible for making accurate premium quotations to prospective insureds.

In some cases, a prospect will call an agent or a broker to inquire about insurance. In others, the agent or broker will make the first contact with the prospect. In either case, at some point the prospect will ask the agent or broker for a **quotation**. The quotation gives the prospect a close approximation of the price, or premium, he or she can expect to pay for the insurance.

Should the prospect decide to buy, an **application** (or "app," for short) must be filled out and sent to the company. The application contains a description of the prospect and the risk to be covered and is signed by the prospect. Based on this information (and sometimes additional information from other sources), the company decides whether or not to insure the prospect and is able to determine the appropriate premium to charge.

The agent or broker may also collect the first premium payment on the coverage. Once the insurance company issues the policy, the insured may continue to pay premiums to the agent or broker, who will then remit them to the insurance company, or the insured may send premiums directly to the insurance company.

   A. An agent gives a prospect information about the price of an insurance policy by means of a _____.

   B. The document that must be completed in order to provide information to the insurance company about the prospect and the risk to be insured is called an _____.

Answer: A. quotation; B. application

6. In some cases, insurance companies give agents, as their legal representatives, the authority to **bind** insurance coverage until they actually issue a policy. (Brokers do not have binding authority because legally they represent the insured rather than the company.) A **binder** is either an oral or written statement by an agent telling the insured that he or she has immediate insurance protection, valid for a specified time.

   Naturally, agents should document oral binders in writing as soon as possible.

   Insurance companies may also issue binders. Insurance companies often do this to let insureds know that they are covered during the period it takes to issue a policy.

Which of the following statements is correct?

   A. Binders are valid only if they are written.

   B. It is not worthwhile to document a binder once it has been given orally.

   C. Binders provide immediate insurance protection that is valid for a specific amount of time.

Answer: C is correct.

7. Regardless of who issues the binder, the agent or the company, a binder provides only temporary coverage. A binder remains in effect only until the insured receives an actual policy.

Alice's agent tells her on March 14 that she is "bound," effective that date for 60 days. She gets the actual policy on March 23. Does the binder apply any longer? ( ) Yes   ( ) No

Answer: No

8. Because the binder provides only temporary coverage, the company has the right to reject an application even after issuing a binder. Although this does not happen frequently, there are times when it may be necessary. In such

a case, the prospect has coverage only until the binder expires or until the company sends official notice of cancellation, whichever is earliest.

Herb receives a document from his agent on July 6 that binds liability coverage for 30 days. However, Herb does not meet all the company's policyholder requirements and after reviewing the application, the company decides not to issue a policy. Herb's agent informs him of the company's decision. However, the insurance company does not formally cancel Herb's binder. On July 26, Herb has an accident for which he is liable. Does he have insurance protection?   ( ) Yes   ( ) No

Answer: Yes

9. If the company agrees to insure the prospect, it prepares a policy. This is often done at the company home office or a regional branch office, but in some cases agents may issue policies themselves. After the policy is issued, the agent or broker must then deliver it to the new insured.

    In some cases, the agent or broker must **countersign** the policy after it is prepared. Countersigning simply means the agent or broker signs each new policy before delivering it to the policyholder. Most states require the agent's or broker's countersignature on the policy to validate the contract.

    In a state with a countersignature requirement, which of the following policies has been properly validated?

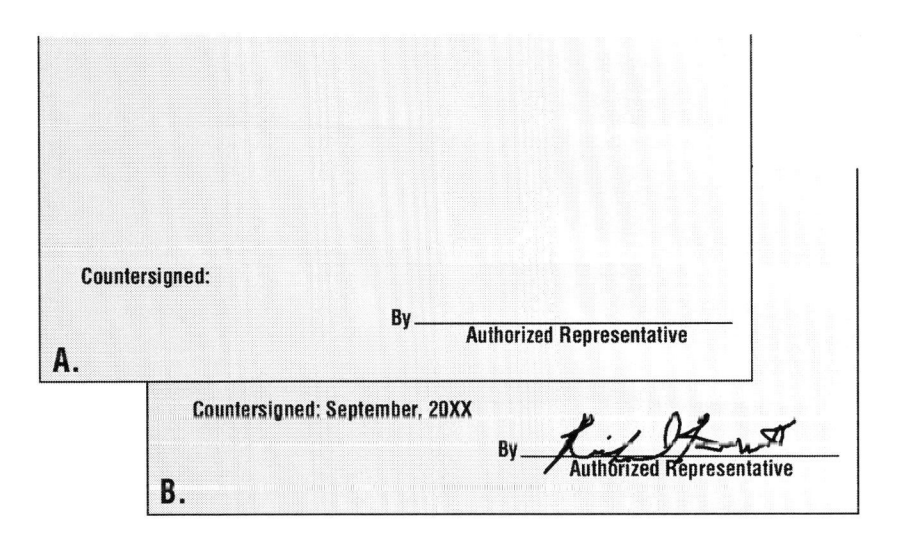

Answer: B is correct.

10. After agents and brokers deliver a policy, they have a continuing service responsibility to their insureds. Prior to the time policies come up for renewal, agents and brokers may review their clients' insurance and make sure it is still adequate. They also assist insureds with service needs, such as changing the address on a policy or changing the method of payment at an insured's request. Agents and brokers may also assist insureds after a loss occurs and a claim must be filed with the company.

In some cases, the insurance company gives agents or brokers the authority to settle claims on its behalf without involving a company claim representative if the amount of the claim doesn't exceed a certain amount. The upper limit on the amount for which an agent or broker may write a company claim check is referred to as the agent's or broker's **draft authority**.

Which of the following may be done by an agent but not a broker?
A. Quote premiums
B. Bind coverage
C. Deliver policies
D. Handle premiums
E. Settle small claims

Answer: B is correct.

Agent Support

11. In agencies, the agents often employ someone, such as an office manager, administrative assistant, or customer service representative, to support their sales and service efforts by providing administrative backup and customer service on existing policies.

Providing Support

Most agents employ an office manager, administrative assistant, or customer service representative to provide administrative support.

Identify who would perform each of the following activities by writing an "A" for agent or an "S" for support person in the blank provided.

____ A. Calls on a prospect to collect all the data necessary to complete an application

____ B. Transfers notes taken in an interview to the actual application form and submits the necessary materials to the insurance company

____ C. Keeps track of which policies are coming up for renewal and pulls the file on those policies in advance of the renewal date

____ D. Reviews an insured's coverage in advance of the renewal date to make sure it is adequate

____ E. Recommends that an insured add new insurance to fill a coverage gap

____ F. Makes routine changes to existing policies at the request of an insured

Answer: A A.; S B.; S C.; A D.; A E.; S F.

Home Office Marketing Functions

12. To market their product, insurance company home offices perform a number of activities. They contract agents to represent the company, provide training and/or sales support materials to agents, analyze consumer needs and product trends, and advertise.

    Some companies consolidate these functions in a single Marketing Department. Other companies may have a different name for this department or may have these functions split among several departments, such as an Agency Department that contracts with agents or a Marketing Services Department that provides various types of home office support to agents. There may also be separate Advertising and Training Departments.

    The heads of these departments are often officers of the company or executives with titles such as Vice President, Director, or Manager. The staff members of these departments perform vital work and help the company fulfill its business goals.

Ask your supervisor how your company organizes its marketing function.

Match the activity with the possible title of the individual who would perform it.

____ A. Manages the marketing function at the home office level

____ B. Supports the activities of the agent, sometimes in direct contact with insureds

____ C. Represents an insurance company to the public

1. Agent
2. Office manager
3. Director of Marketing

Answer: 3 A.; 2 B.; 1 C.

UNDERWRITING

13. **Underwriting** is the process of evaluating the risks involved in insuring a particular individual or business. The Underwriting Department is made up of many individual **underwriters** who decide whether to accept or reject applications submitted to the company, based on the company's written standards and their own experienced judgment. Underwriting departments may be organized by territory, by product or type of insurance, or by type of customer (small businesses, large businesses, individuals, etc.). While insurance companies are in the business of accepting risks, it is the underwriter's job to ensure that the company doesn't accept risks that are uninsurable or that bear an unacceptably high chance of loss in relation to the premium charged for the coverage.

The Underwriter's Job

Underwriters are responsible for determining whether a proposed risk meets the company's standards.

An underwriter's job is to
A. accept only those applications that represent no risk.
B. accept any risk.
C. accept only those risks that are insurable and acceptable to the company.

Answer: C is correct.

Sources of Information

14. In considering each application, underwriters may draw on other sources of information to help them evaluate the risk, such as the following:

    - Inspection services
    - Government bureaus, such as the Bureau of Motor Vehicles
    - Insurance bureaus, such as the National Fire Protection Association
    - Financial information services such as Standard and Poor's or Dun & Bradstreet
    - The company's own files

    Which of the following statements correctly describes the sources of information an underwriter may consult regarding a given risk?
    A. The underwriter's job begins and ends with the application.
    B. The underwriter can make a decision based on other sources of information without considering the application itself.
    C. The underwriter may consult a number of sources of information in addition to the application.

Answer: C is correct.

Regulations Govern the Use of Information

15. Certain regulations exist to protect consumers from the potential for abuse. For example, the Fair Credit Reporting Act states that if a consumer is denied insurance because of information contained in a credit report dealing with the prospect's credit rating, general reputation, or personal character, the consumer must be notified. Further, the consumer must be allowed to obtain the file information from the reporting agency. This gives the consumer an opportunity to refute the report and have it corrected if the evidence shows that it contains inaccurate data.

    The Fair Credit Reporting Act
    A. forbids underwriters from using inspection services or credit bureaus in evaluating risks.
    B. limits the number of outside sources an underwriter may use in evaluating a risk.
    C. gives the consumer recourse should insurance be denied on the basis of a credit report.
    D. permits the use of installment payments for insurance premiums.

Answer: C is correct.

Hazards Are Important Factors

16. One factor that is very important to underwriters in evaluating potential insureds is **hazard**. A hazard is anything that increases the *chance* of loss.

    You should distinguish this term in your mind from the word **peril**, which is a *cause* of loss.

    For example, faulty brakes are a *hazard* that increase the chance of collision (a *peril*).

    Here's another example that distinguishes a hazard from a peril.

Hazard Versus Peril

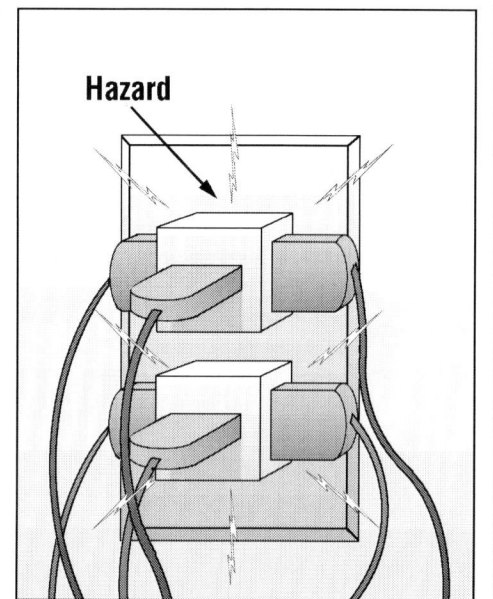

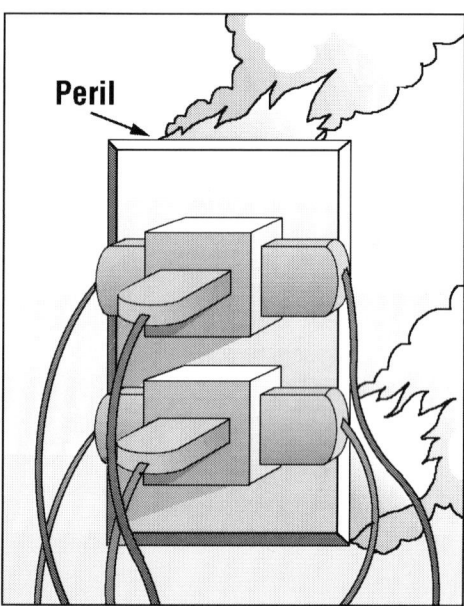

Identify the hazards (H) and the perils (P) in the following descriptions.
   ____ A. Leaving your doors unlocked
   ____ B. Theft
   ____ C. Fire
   ____ D. Improper storage of flammable materials

Answer: H A.; P B.; P C.; H D.

17. Because we cope with many hazards every day, insurance technicians are concerned with hazards. They realize that reducing hazards can, in turn, reduce the occurrence of losses that have to be indemnified.
    A. In your opinion, can perils ever be completely eliminated?
       ( ) Yes, of course   ( ) No, probably not
    B. Can measures be taken which will reduce the hazards associated with various perils?   ( ) Yes, of course   ( ) No, probably not

Answer: A. No, probably not; B. Yes, of course

18. Insurance companies are very safety conscious. They try to reduce hazards among their insureds, but they also try to select risks that have fewer hazards associated with them.

    Hazards can be subdivided into three major categories. One type is the **morale hazard**. This is a hazard whereby people, through carelessness or by their own irresponsible actions, can increase the possibility of a loss.

    Which of the following examples demonstrates possible morale hazards?
    A. Aileen operates a dynamite factory. She is very safety conscious—inspects her plant regularly and complies with every safety requirement.
    B. Jonas feels that insurance protects him, so he sees no need to check the driveway in back of his car before he backs out.
    C. The ABC Gas Company has, for years, had an employee who smokes while refilling propane gas cylinders. Nothing disastrous has happened in this time.

    Answer: B and C are correct.

19. A second type of hazard, which is closely related to the morale hazard, is the **moral hazard**. This involves a situation in which a person might create a loss on purpose in order to collect from an insurance company.

    Identify the types of hazards in the following examples.
    A. Jerry is having serious business difficulties. He plans to burn down the building in which his business operated so he can collect on the fire insurance. This is a (morale/moral) _____ hazard.
    B. Bill leaves his car unlocked whenever he goes shopping. He figures that the car is insured and there is no reason to worry. This is a (morale/moral) _____ hazard.
    C. Mary wants a new fur coat. She makes the necessary arrangements and "conveniently" leaves her old fur coat in a bus station so that someone will take it. This is a (morale/moral) _____ hazard.

    Answer: A. moral; B. morale; C. moral

20. A third type of hazard, **physical hazard**, arises from the condition, occupancy, or use of the property itself. This is apart from the character of the individual associated with the property (which would involve moral or morale hazards).

Write the type of hazard present—physical, moral, or morale—next to the following examples.

A. Lewis manufactures fireworks in the back room of a furniture warehouse. In ten years, only two major explosions have occurred, a record for the fireworks industry. _____

B. The Starfire Equipment Company has had several serious fires in the last two years. It occupies a very old building near the center of town. An inspector recently said that a worn-out furnace may be the reason for these fires. _____

C. Pat, a doctor, is very involved with her work. Her mind tends to wander and she thinks about her patients when she is driving. _____

D. The Evertite Screen Door company is having serious financial problems. Evertite's president begins thinking about having a small fire in a room to get rid of some worthless, left over stock. She thinks she'll tell the insurance company that the stock was worth much more than its actual value. _____

Answer: A. physical; B. physical; C. morale; D. moral

Underwriting Authority

21. Insurance companies generally give their underwriters a limit on the amount of risk they accept on behalf of the company. This limit is referred to as **underwriting authority**. If the amount of coverage to be provided to an insured or the amount of premium to be charged for that coverage exceeds an underwriter's authority, a supervisor must review the case and approve the recommendation. If the case exceeds the supervisor's underwriting authority, the supervisor's manager must review and approve the recommendation, and so on, up the line of underwriting management.

    John is an underwriter. If he evaluates a case that calls for more than $250,000 of coverage or more than $25,000 of annual premium, his supervisor must review the recommendation. The $250,000 of coverage/$25,000 annual premium limit is known as John's _____.

Answer: underwriting authority

Underwriting Management

22. In addition to deciding whether to accept or reject cases that represent potentially large risks to the company, underwriting management also decides the general types of risks the company is willing to insure. For example, after analyzing its claims experience with various types of industries, underwriting

management might decide that it has special expertise in underwriting agricultural operations, but that it wishes to limit the company's exposure to them. Guidelines such as these are written in an **underwriting manual** so that individual underwriters can follow them when they make their decisions.

John, an underwriter, is considering an application to insure a small airline. One of the places he could check to see if his insurance company wants to insure this type of business is the company's _____.

Answer: underwriting manual

The Role of Reinsurance

23. Insurance companies must, by law, keep a lot of money in reserve to pay for large losses. But even with this reserve, a catastrophic loss could put a severe strain on a company. To protect itself against having to bear the risk of a single, large loss, an insurance company will give part of the premium on a very large policy to another insurance company, or perhaps more than one, in return for its agreement to assume part of the risk. This process is known as **reinsurance**. Underwriting management helps decide in what cases and in what amounts reinsurance is desirable.

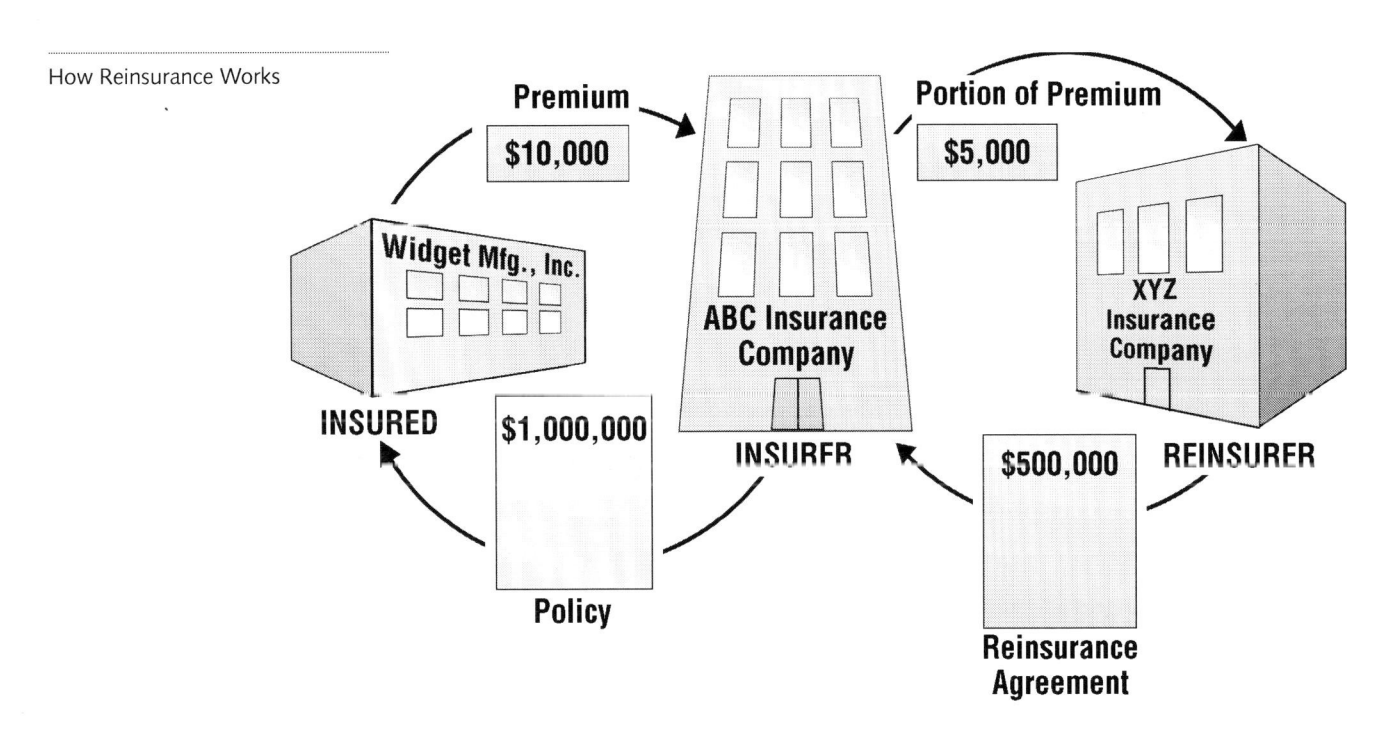

How Reinsurance Works

Select the example of reinsurance from the following descriptions.

A. Insurance company A insures a new office building for $10 million. It has an agreement with insurance company B to pay $5 million of the claim if a total loss occurs.

B. An insurance company insures a new hotel for $2 million. If there is a total loss, that company will pay the entire claim itself.

Answer: A is correct.

24. State laws often require that an insurance company reinsure a portion of its large risks. This prevents a company from going bankrupt if a large loss should occur. Look at reinsurance as a device for spreading the risk of a single large loss among a number of insurance companies.

There are a couple of different methods of spreading the risk among insurance companies through reinsurance. Under one method, the company that initially wrote the policy (the **ceding** company) retains any loss up to a certain amount. The company that has agreed to share the risk (the **reinsurer**) agrees to pay the remaining amount of any claim.

Insurance company A wrote an $8 million policy and retained $4 million of the risk. Insurance company B agreed to pay up to $4 million of losses under the policy, but only after insurance company A has paid its full $4 million. A $3 million loss occurred.

A. How much of the loss will insurance company A pay? $_____
B. How much of the loss will insurance company B pay? $_____
C. Suppose a $6 million loss occurred. How much would insurance company A pay? $_____
D. How much of a $6 million loss would insurance company B pay? $_____

Answer: A. $3 million; B. 0; C. $4 million; D. $2 million

25. Another way of spreading the risk among insurers is for each insurance company to agree to pay a prorated share of any loss.

A. Insurance company A and insurance company B have a reinsurance agreement that calls for payment of any loss in equal shares. If a $2 million loss occurs, how much will insurance company A pay? $_____
B. How much will insurance company B pay? $_____
C. Suppose the loss were for $3 million. How much would each company pay? $_____

Answer: A. $1 million; B. $1 million; C. $1.5 million

RATING, RATES, AND PREMIUMS

26. In addition to accepting or rejecting risks, underwriters have some responsibility for pricing a product—that is, determining the premium that will be charged to the customer. The process of calculating a premium is called **rating**. Depending on how a company is organized and the complexity of a product, rating may be done by the underwriter or assigned to a **rating clerk**, who may be part of the Underwriting Department or part of the Policy Issue or Policy Administration Department.

The Rater's Job

Raters calculate premiums for policies.

Rating Methods

Manual Rating

27. There are three basic rating methods. The most common is **manual rating**, also known as **class rating.** In this method, insurance companies group insureds by class according to certain common risk characteristics. Rates are based on actual loss experience for insureds in each class. The rates for each class are contained in a manual—which these days is usually stored on a computer—and these rates are used to calculate the premium for each insured. In manual rating, the basic formula used to establish the premium is:

$$\text{Rate} \times \text{Exposure Units} = \text{Premium}$$

If a rate is $.30 for each unit of exposure and there are 100 units, how much is the premium? $_____

Answer: $30

Experience Rating

28. Another means for determining premiums is known as **experience** or **merit rating**. Generally, the experience rating calculation begins with a premium that is derived by manual rating. Then a discount or a surcharge is applied to the premium to account for past loss experience, typically over the last three years.

    The Ezra Toy Company has had fewer-than-average losses compared to other companies in its industry. Consequently, it qualifies for a discount from the manual premium. This is an example of _____ rating.

    Answer: merit

Judgment Rating

29. The oldest form of rating is called **judgment rating**. With judgment rating, a premium is determined based upon an individual evaluation of the risk. No books or tables are used. There is no past experience, just the premium selected after careful judgment. Unique risks may require judgment rating.

    Select the example of judgment rating from the descriptions below.
    A. The premium for automobile insurance is determined from the rates previously approved by each state.
    B. A famous pianist would like to obtain insurance protection against the loss of his fingers. The insurance company determines that the premium is $10,000 for three years.
    C. The future premium for fire insurance to protect the Acme Fence Company is determined after the policy has been in effect for one year. The premium is determined based on the number and size of losses that Acme had during that year.

    Answer: B is correct.

Establishing Rates

30. You may be wondering how insurance companies establish manual rates in the first place. The calculations required to develop insurance rates are very

complex and are generally performed by an **actuary**. Actuaries are specialists in the mathematical formulas and statistics that relate to insurance rates and premiums. Actuaries are often part of a separate Actuarial Department that supports the Underwriting Department and other departments in their job of deciding what risks to accept, how to price products, and so on.

The key component of an insurance rate is **loss costs**. Loss costs are based on historical data and show companies how much they need to collect in premiums just to cover expected losses. Some companies calculate loss costs based on their own past experience. However, many companies join organizations, or bureaus, in which members pool their loss data—as you'll recall from our discussion of the law of large numbers, a larger pool of data allows for more accurate predictions of future experience. These organizations then develop loss costs that all members of the organization can use. The largest such organization is the **Insurance Services Office (ISO)**, which also develops standard policy forms for members' use.

Developing Insurance Rates

Actuaries are mathematical specialists who help develop insurance rates.

Once loss costs are established, other factors are taken into account in determining the final rate. Insurance companies may increase the rate to cover operating expenses, for example, or reduce it to account for investment income. Insurance companies must do all of this with an eye toward developing a final rate that is adequate, not excessive, and not unfairly discriminatory, as we discussed in the Rate Regulation section of Unit 3.

Ask your supervisor if your company develops its own loss costs or uses those developed by a service organization.

A. Loss costs are (equal to/a key component of) _____ an insurance company's rates.

B. All companies develop their own loss costs. ( ) True ( ) False

Answer: A. a key component of; B. False

Premium Terms

31. Before leaving our discussion of rates and premiums, there are a few related terms you should know.

Minimum Premium

Every company has certain items of expense that are necessary to sell and process insurance. On some policies with low premiums it could cost the company more to issue the policy than the amount of the premium. And that's before the insurance company pays any claims! For that reason, it is sometimes necessary to charge a **minimum premium**.

Select the example where a minimum premium would apply.

A. According to the rating manual, insurance for a particular camera will be $7.50 per year. However, to issue any policy of this type, the company must charge at least $10 for the coverage.

B. A rating clerk computes an automobile insurance premium to be $253, above the minimum premium of $75.

Answer: A is correct.

Written/Earned/Unearned Premium

32. Insureds generally pay premiums in advance for a year's (or sometimes six months') worth of coverage. When an insurance company collects the premium, it is referred to as being **written**. This term is generally used in connection with financial statements, where it denotes the total number of premium dollars received by a company.

In the first quarter of this year, ABC Insurance Company collected a total of $1 million in premiums from its insureds. Written premium for the first quarter of this year would be _____.

Answer: $1 million

33. However, even though a premium has been collected, the company still has to *earn* it. The company has **earned premium** to the extent that it has provided insurance coverage for some period of time.

   Let's say that one month ago you paid a $600 premium for six months of automobile insurance coverage.
   A. What is the written premium on your policy? $_____
   B. What is the earned premium on your policy at this point? $_____
   C. How much of the written premium is left for the company to earn? $_____

Answer: A. $600; B. $100; C. $500

34. Premium written, but not yet earned, is **unearned premium**.

Written Premium/Earned Premium/Unearned Premium

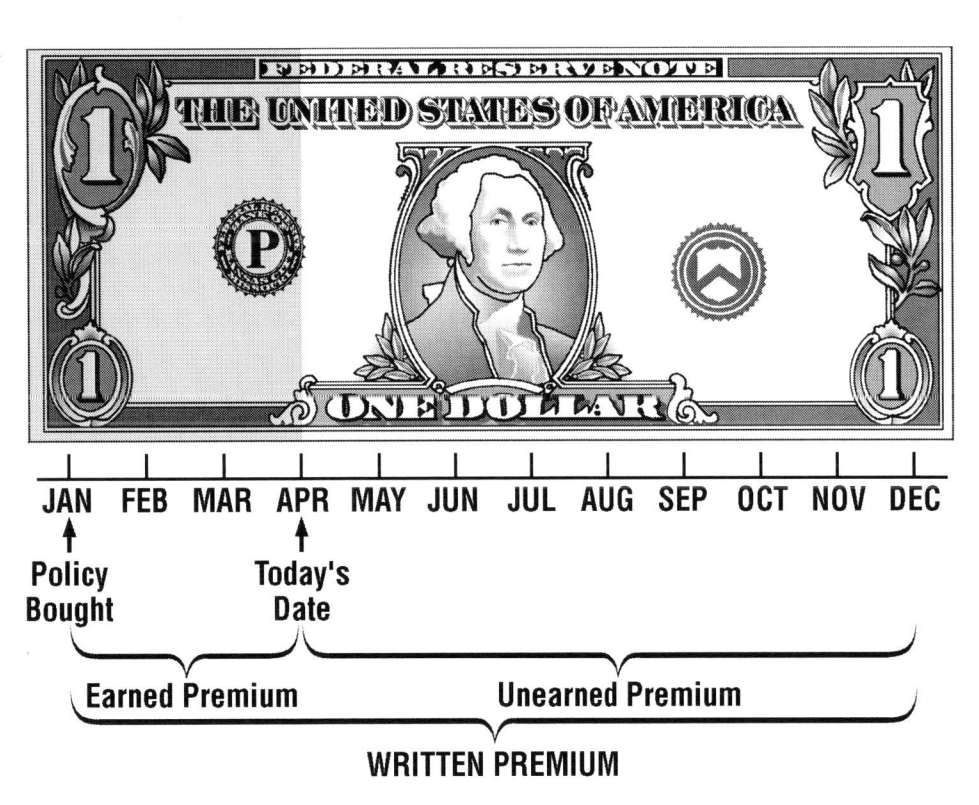

| JAN   FEB   MAR   APR   MAY   JUN   JUL   AUG   SEP   OCT   NOV   DEC
   ↑   ↑
Policy   Today's
Bought   Date

Earned Premium (JAN–APR) | Unearned Premium (APR–DEC)
WRITTEN PREMIUM

Let's say that you reach the end of the policy period and pay another $600 to renew your coverage.

A. Regarding the renewal premium, how much is written premium?
$_____
B. How much of the renewal premium has the insurance company earned at this point? $_____
C. How much of the renewal premium is unearned at this point?
$_____
D. At the end of the policy period, how much of the premium will be unearned? $_____
E. Because some insureds cancel their policies before the end of the policy period, you would expect a company's earned premiums to be (less than/equal to) _____ its written premiums.

Answer: A. $600; B. $0; C. $600; D. $0; E. less than

Provisional Premium/Audited Premium

35. The premiums for some coverages are based on units of exposure that can't be known in advance. For example, a policy that covers a business may have a premium based on the size of the business's payroll. Since the business may hire or terminate employees during the year, there's no way of telling exactly what the business's payroll will be over the coverage period.

    In such cases, insurance companies compute a **provisional premium** that is payable in advance. The provisional premium is based on factors that provide a "best guess" about the number of exposure units the company will be insuring over the policy period. At the end of the policy period, the insurance company's **premium auditor** examines the insured's financial records to determine the actual number of exposure units for that period. The **audited premium** is then computed. If the audited premium exceeds the provisional premium, the insured pays an additional amount to the company. If the audited premium is less than the provisional premium, the insurance company refunds a portion of the premium to the business.

    The provisional premium paid by the Hart Company was based on an annual payroll of $500,000. At the end of the policy period, a premium auditor determined that the Hart Company's actual payroll was $525,000. In this case, the audited premium will be (greater than/less than/equal to) _____ the provisional premium.

    Answer: greater than

POLICY ISSUE/ADMINISTRATION/SERVICE

36. Once an application for insurance has been accepted and the policy has been rated, it must be printed and sent either to the insured or to the producer for delivery. In some companies, this function is performed by a separate department, called Policy Issue, Policy Administration or Policy Service. In other companies, it may be a part of the Underwriting Department.

Policy Issue

In the policy issue/administration/service area, **data entry technicians** ensure that the correct information about insureds is entered onto policy forms. **Policy typists** prepare any specialized documents that must accompany the standard policy forms. Then **policy issue clerks**, also known as **policy analysts** or **screeners**, make sure that the proper policy documents are assembled and mailed. Later, if information in a policy needs to be revised—such as on an auto policy if an insured buys a new car—a clerk in this department will handle the change.

CLAIMS

Fair Settlement

37. Insurance companies deliver on the promises they make in their policies by paying claims. To be fair to insureds who suffer losses, companies must deliver fully on their promises. At the same time, to be fair to those insureds

who have not suffered losses, but whose premiums reflect the cost of losses, companies must be careful not to pay for losses that their policies don't cover. They also must be careful not to pay more for losses than they legitimately owe.

The goal of claims settlement is to

A. pay the full amount asked on any claim filed, no questions asked.
B. deny payment even on legitimate claims in order to save the company money.
C. pay all that is owed, but no more than is owed.

Answer: C is correct.

Claim Representatives

Claim Handling

Claim representatives work with insureds and third-party claimants to settle claims.

38. The people who work with insureds and third-party claimants to settle claims are called **claim representatives**, or sometimes claim handlers or claim adjusters. Claim representatives are part of the Claim Department, the managers of which set claim policy, assign claims to claim representatives, and monitor the flow of claim activity. There are four types of claim representatives:

- **Staff claim representatives** are employees of the insurance company who investigate claims and negotiate settlements with insureds or third-party claimants. Sometimes these claim representatives work entirely from inside their office, by phone and mail. These claim representatives may be called **telephone claim representatives, inside adjusters** or **office adjusters**. A **field claim representative**, sometimes called an **outside adjuster**, goes on-site to inspect damage and conduct other claims settlement activities.

- **Independent adjusters** are independent contractors who specialize in claims settlement. Most companies use staff adjusters to handle the majority of their claims and hire independent adjusters only in special circumstances—if the claims workload is especially heavy, if a claim requires certain expertise possessed by a particular independent adjuster, or for claims in locations that are removed from the companies usual area of operations, for example.

Ask your supervisor how your company organizes its claim function.

- **Bureau adjusters** are not employed by an insurance company, nor are they independent adjusters. They are employed by a bureau organization that offers claim handling services to member insurance companies for a fee.

- **Public adjusters** are individuals (other than attorneys) who may be hired by insureds to represent them in the settlement of a claim with an insurer.

Identify each of the following types of adjusters by writing "staff," "independent," "bureau," or "public" in the blank provided.

A. When her business suffers extensive loss because of an accidental fire, Mary wants to make sure nothing is overlooked in regard to her insurance claim, so she hires adjuster Adams to represent her in regard to the settlement with the company. _____

B. When an earthquake strikes a metropolitan area, the ABC Insurance Company hires the Willdooh Adjustment Firm to help handle the heavy claims caseload. _____

C. When fire destroys an insured's home, the S&T Insurance Company sends its employee, Dan Couch, to inspect the damage and issue a check to the insured to cover the immediate expenses of moving into other temporary living quarters. _____

D. When a hail storm damages a number of insureds' cars, the L&D Insurance Company pays an organization to which it belongs a fee for claim handling services. _____

Answer: A. public; B. independent; C. staff; D. bureau

Reserving

39. A period of time is usually required between the filing and the settlement of a claim to investigate the claim and determine the cause and extent of the loss. However, as soon as the company has an indication that it will pay something on a claim, even though the actual amount may be unknown, it sets aside a **loss reserve** against the payment of the claim. In establishing the loss reserve, the company estimates the total amount it expects to pay on the claim, based on what it knows about the claim at that point. Loss reserves are revised as new information is learned about the claim. Loss reserving helps a company more accurately assess the impact of future claims on its financial picture, even before those claims come due.

Bert leaves his car outdoors in a hailstorm. When he calls his insurance company, he reports that no glass was broken, but the metal body is battered all over. He makes an appointment to meet with an adjuster the next day. From the company's claim experience, it can be estimated that damage such as Bert described on a car such as his will cost $4,000 to repair. At this point the company will do which of the following?

A. Write a check to Bert for $4,000.
B. Set aside a loss reserve of $4,000.
C. Nothing until the adjuster can verify the damage.

Answer: B is correct.

Regulations

40. The states have passed laws to protect consumers against unfair claim practices. Companies must adhere, and make sure their claim handlers adhere, to certain standards in settling claims. For example, individuals are entitled to receive a prompt response—usually within a time limit specified by law—to inquiries or communications involving a claim. The law requires companies to keep records of the numbers and types of complaints they receive about claims and how those complaints were handled.

Dan calls his insurer to report a claim after lightning strikes his house. It (is/is not) _____ important for the insurer to make sure that a claim form is sent to Dan promptly.

Answer: is

OTHER INSURANCE FUNCTIONS

41. At this point you have an idea of the basic functions that are required to make insurance protection available to the public. There are many other people whose jobs are essential to an insurance company's operation.

Loss Prevention and Control

- In a Loss Prevention and Control Department, **loss control specialists** or **engineers** inspect insured premises with an eye toward preventing losses from happening. These individuals make recommendations to insureds about how they can avoid or reduce losses. They may also work with claim handlers to determine the causes of losses and help prevent recurrences.

- In an Accounting Department, **bookkeepers** keep track of premiums due and paid on policies, commissions due and paid to agents, and other financial transactions. Bookkeepers in the home office work with bookkeepers in the agencies to make sure everyone's records reconcile properly. In addition, the states closely regulate the financial condition of insurance companies. Therefore, insurance companies must maintain records of income and expenses according to strict accounting standards. Premiums are credited to specific lines of insurance, and proper reserves must be computed and maintained.

Accounting

Investment

- In an Investment Department, **investment specialists** are responsible for investing the company's funds in such a way that they earn a healthy return while ensuring adequate safety over the long term and adequate liquidity in the short term. For example, highly speculative investments are generally not appropriate, and some investments must be readily convertible to cash. As with accounting, the investment practices of insurance companies are carefully regulated.

Legal

- In a Legal Department, **staff attorneys** handle many tasks that require legal expertise. Policies are legal contracts, so they are drafted with input from attorneys. Attorneys also help interpret applicable local, state, and federal laws and help make sure that the company complies with those laws. In addition, they give advice or represent the company in court when lawsuits arise from claims, but only in cases where the attorney can fairly represent the interests of both the company and the insured.

Operational Support

- Numerous other departments support a company's operations. For example, a **Personnel** or **Human Resources Department** ensures that the company recruits quality people for all its various positions. An **Information Services** or **Data Processing Department** is responsible for providing adequate computer support for all company operations. A **Mail Operations Department** ensures a timely and efficient flow of documents throughout the home office and between the home office and the agencies. A **Building and Maintenance Department** helps establish a working environment that enables everyone to do their jobs effectively.

For each of the examples given, identify who handles the function described.

A. An applicant is accepted for auto insurance after an evaluation of information related to the risk. _____

B. A policy premium is computed based on information in the insured's application. _____

C. An inspection of an insured's financial records is made to determine the premium for coverage at the end of the policy term. _____

D. An insured's factory is inspected, and recommendations about a worker safety program are made to an insured. _____

E. An insured's home is inspected to determine the extent of a loss. _____

Answer: A. underwriter; B. rater; C. premium auditor; D. loss control specialist or engineer; E. claim handler

TEAMS

42. The various departments in an insurance company interact to make insurance protection available to the public. Some companies form teams of individuals from various departments to work together on customer accounts. For example, a team might be composed of an underwriter, a sales representative, a rater, and possibly a claims person and a loss control specialist all serving a single geographic area or a single type of customer or line of insurance. Having all these individuals working together on an account ensures accurate communication and efficient delivery of the company's promises to the insured.

Ask your supervisor whether your company uses teams.

In a team, who is responsible for evaluating the extent to which an insured meets the company's standards and can be accepted? _____

Answer: the underwriter

You now have an idea of the various functions carried out by an insurance company and the people who perform them. In the next unit, we will take a general look at the product that all these people are working to provide to the public: the insurance contract.

UNIT 5

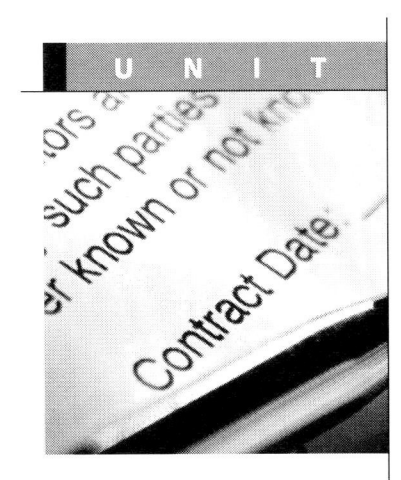

The Insurance Contract

1. In this unit, we'll talk about insurance policy structure. While there are many different types of insurance coverages, most insurance policies contain the same basic elements. In addition, we'll talk about some of the ways insurance policies can be classified. More specifically, we'll cover:

    - the characteristics that make an insurance policy a special kind of legal contract;
    - the four major parts of an insurance policy;
    - the types of losses that insurance policies protect people against;
    - the main types of losses that are excluded from insurance policies;
    - the most common conditions included in insurance policies; and
    - the various ways in which insurance policies may be categorized.

    The material in this unit will get you ready for the next one, which describes a number of specific property-casualty insurance policies.

CHARACTERISTICS OF CONTRACTS

2. A **contract** is a legally binding agreement between two parties who wish to exchange some sort of **consideration** (consideration is anything of value, such as money or goods). In the case of an insurance policy, the two parties are the **insurer** and the **insured**. The consideration that the insurer gives is the promise to pay for certain losses suffered by the insured. The consideration that the insured gives is the premium.

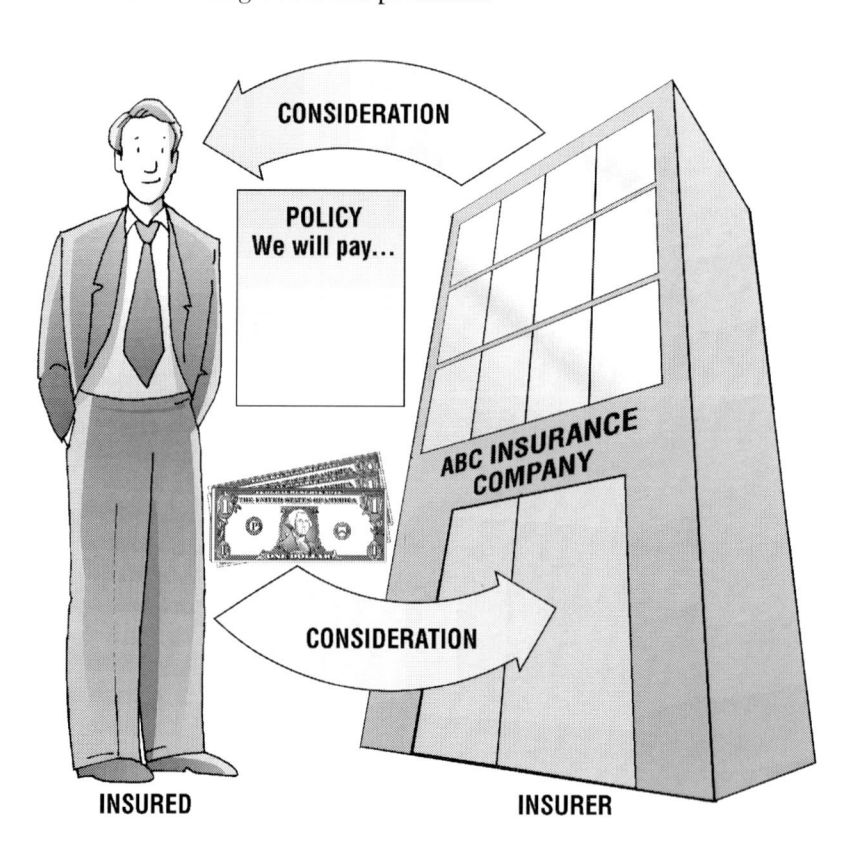

The Insurance Contract

For $500, John buys an insurance policy from ABC Insurance Company that promises to indemnify him in the event his house burns. Identify the elements of this contract.

A. Who is the insured? _____

B. Who is the insurer? _____

C. What consideration is given by ABC Insurance Company?
   _____

D. What consideration is given by John? _____

Answer: A. John; B. ABC Insurance Company; C. the promise to indemnify John in the event of fire losses to his house; D. $500

3. An insurance policy has some characteristics that make it a special kind of contract. For example:

   ■ An insurance policy is a **unilateral contract**. "Unilateral" means "one-sided." An insurance policy is one-sided because only the insurance company is legally bound to perform its part of the agreement. If an insured pays a premium and a loss occurs, the insurer is legally bound to pay for the loss under the terms of the policy. However, insureds are not legally obligated to pay premiums. If insureds stop paying premiums, the insurance company can cancel coverage, but it can't take them to court for breaking the contract. On the other hand, if an insured fails to comply with conditions and duties specified in the contract, the insurance company may sometimes deny an insured's claims.

   ■ An insurance policy is an **aleatory contract**. "Aleatory" means that the insurer's obligation to pay is based on a **contingency** (an event that is not certain to occur). If insureds do not suffer a covered loss, they will not get any claims money. In such cases, what insureds are considered to receive in return for their premiums is "peace of mind"—the knowledge that they are covered if any loss should occur. On the other hand, insureds who suffer a loss often get many more dollars back in claims than they've paid in premiums.

   ■ An insurance policy is a **contract of adhesion**. This means that the terms of the contract are drawn up by only one of the parties (in this case, the insurer). Because insureds don't have any input, courts will usually interpret any unclear wording in an insurance policy in their favor.

   Label the following as being characteristic of a unilateral contract, an aleatory contract, or a contract of adhesion.

   A. George pays a $200 premium. He does not suffer a covered loss, so he gets no money back in claims. _____

   B. The policy Harold bought from XYZ Insurance Company isn't clear about whether it covers a loss he experienced, so a judge rules that XYZ must indemnify Harold for the loss. _____

   C. Agnes decides to drop the policy covering her car; the insurance company refunds the unearned premium to her. _____

Answer: A. aleatory contract; B. contract of adhesion; C. unilateral contract

STANDARDIZATION OF POLICIES

4. In the early days of insurance, policy wording varied from company to company, even from insured to insured. Today, though, policies have been standardized somewhat. As we mentioned when we covered insurance regulation, certain policies have been standardized by law. A degree of standardization has also been introduced by insurance organizations, such as the Insurance Services Office (you'll recall we mentioned ISO earlier).

   Which of the following statements is correct?
   A. There is no standardization in insurance policies from company to company.
   B. Insurance organizations, such as ISO, promote standardization by creating and filing standard policies on behalf of member companies.
   C. Some policy wording is standardized by law.

   Answer: B and C are correct.

5. The use of standard policies saves companies from having to develop their own individualized policies. But there are benefits other than convenience.
   An insurance policy is a legal contract. The wording of these policies has been interpreted by law over and over. When an insurance company uses a standard policy, rather than a unique policy, it can be fairly certain about how a court will interpret its various provisions.

   What are two benefits to companies of using standardized policies?
   A. _____
   B. _____

   Answer: A. Convenience; B. Greater certainty about the way courts will interpret the wording (either order)

Easy-to-Read/Simplified Policies

6. Because policies are legal contracts, the earliest standard policies were filled with "legalese"—very technical, legal language. While such contracts may have been clear to the company and the courts, they were not clear to the insured.

Many of the policies in use today have replaced this legalese with language that is more direct and easier to understand. The insurance company is called "we" or "us." The named insured is called "you." Even the print size in these policies is larger. These policies are sometimes referred to as **easy-to-read** policies. Easy-to-read policies were first introduced in **personal lines** (insurance designed for individuals and families). The concept later expanded into the **commercial lines** (insurance designed for businesses).

Which of the following statements are true of the easy-to-read or simplified policy forms?

A. They use wording that is easier for insureds to understand.

B. They use larger type.

C. They are not legal contracts.

Answer: A and B are correct.

CLASSIFICATIONS OF POLICIES

Participating/Nonparticipating Policies

7. Besides being classified as either personal or commercial, property-casualty policies may fall into several other types of categories. We will discuss some of them in the remainder of this unit.

Participating Policy

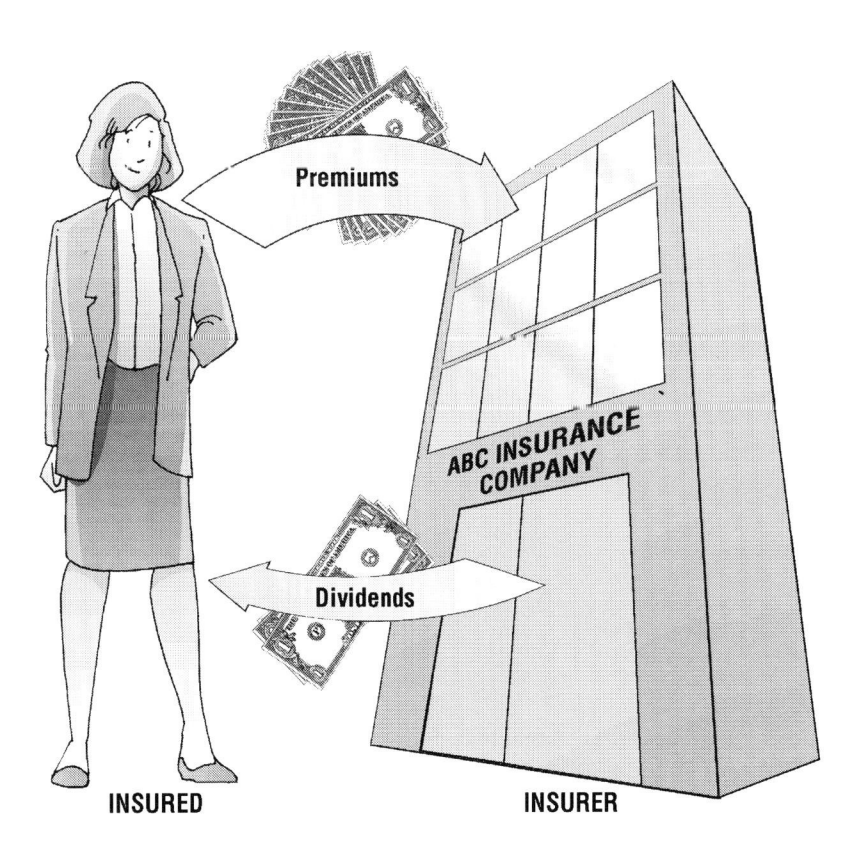

Sometimes, insurers collect more in premium than they need to pay claims and other expenses. If a company issues **participating policies**, then it will return some of the money not needed to the insured. The money returned is called a **dividend**. If a policy is **nonparticipating**, the insured will not receive a dividend.

Identify the examples below as being participating ("P") or nonparticipating ("N").

____ A. Mr. McClure receives a dividend check at the end of the year when the insurance company's income exceeds the amount required to pay claims and expenses.

____ B. Rather than taking a dividend in cash, an insured had the amount of the dividend deducted from his next year's premium.

____ C. Joe Banks owns stock in ABC Insurance Company. He also is a policyholder in that company. When the company has a good year, he receives dividends on his stock, but never on his policy.

Answer: P A.; P B.; N C.

Contracts of Indemnity/Valued Contracts

8. In general, insurance policies are **contracts of indemnity**. That is, in accordance with the principle of indemnity, the amount paid to an insured is based on the amount of a loss. The insurer calculates the amount to be paid after a loss occurs.

    But for certain types of property, such as stamp collections, jewels, furs, or antiques, it's difficult to determine the property's value after it has been damaged or destroyed. So this type of property requires a policy with a special valuation clause. Then it is a **valued policy**.

    In a valued policy, the insured and the insurance company agree to a specific value for the property before the company issues the policy. Then if the property is lost or destroyed, the insured collects the agreed-upon amount.

    Now, see if you can select the valued policy from the following examples.

    A. Joe has insurance on his car that protects him up to $50,000 for damage he might do someone else.

    B. Norma has insured a valuable coin collection. If the entire collection is lost or stolen, she will collect $5,000.

    Answer: B is correct.

9. In agreeing upon the value of an item or group of items to be insured under a valued policy, the insurance company might ask to see the original sales receipt, or the insurer might want to have the property appraised. This evaluation would take place before the company issues the policy.

What two things might be used by the insured and insurance company in setting a value on property to be covered under a valued policy?

A. _____

B. _____

Answer: A. Original sales receipt; B. Appraisal (either order)

Fixed Coverage/Floater Coverage

10. Some insurance is written to cover property at one fixed location. A good example of this is fire insurance on a house. Other kinds of insurance are designed to protect property that moves around. This "moving" insurance is sometimes called a **floater**.

    Select the examples of floaters from the following list.

    A. A fire policy is written to protect the property at 1718 LaFoote Road.
    B. A policy protects the costumes and sets of the Galieg Burlesque Troope as it travels from show to show.
    C. Mrs. Atwater insures her mink coat against loss, regardless of where she might go.
    D. The Acme Brick Company buys insurance under which it would be indemnified if the main building should be destroyed by an explosion.

Answer: B and C are correct.

Reporting/Nonreporting Policies

11. Property insurance contracts may be issued on a **reporting** or **nonreporting** basis. For nonreporting policies, insureds are charged a flat premium every time the policy is renewed. Your car insurance or your homeowners policy are examples of nonreporting-type policies.

    Policies are issued on a reporting basis when it is difficult to determine in advance what amount of coverage should be purchased. Instead of paying a flat premium, the insured pays a deposit and then submits reports to the insurer periodically (monthly, usually) showing the status of those factors on which the premium is based. After the insurance company has calculated the premium, it is charged against the deposit.

    When the deposit is used up, the insured begins to pay the premium calculated by the insurance company at the end of each reporting period.

    Which of the following is a reporting policy?

    A. Maryann receives the insurance policy for her home and a premium due notice of $225.
    B. Darla has purchased an insurance policy for her business. She has paid a deposit up front and will be submitting monthly reports to the insurance company, which will be used to calculate the final premium.

Answer: B is correct.

Monoline/Package Policies

12. Some insurance policies insure against one type of loss—for instance, property loss or liability loss. These policies are sometimes called **monoline** policies. Other policies are designed to insure several categories of loss or provide several lines of insurance within a single contract. These are known as **multiline** or **package** policies. One important personal lines package policy is the **Homeowners** policy. This policy provides two separate lines of coverage—property and liability—in a single package that is designed to meet the insurance needs of homeowners. Another important package policy is the **Commercial Package policy (CPP)**, which allows various coverages to be selected and combined into a single policy covering a business. Package policies provide cost savings for the insurance company, and the company may pass these savings along to the insured as package discounts that reduce the policy premium.

    Which of the following is a package policy?
    A. Marvin purchases burglary insurance for his business.
    B. Caroline purchases a policy from ABC Insurance Company that provides her business with both property and liability insurance coverage.

Answer: B is correct.

SECTIONS OF A POLICY

Four Basic Parts

13. Because an insurance policy is a legal contract, the agreements it contains must be spelled out carefully. To help keep things organized, most policies have four parts.

The Four Parts of a Policy

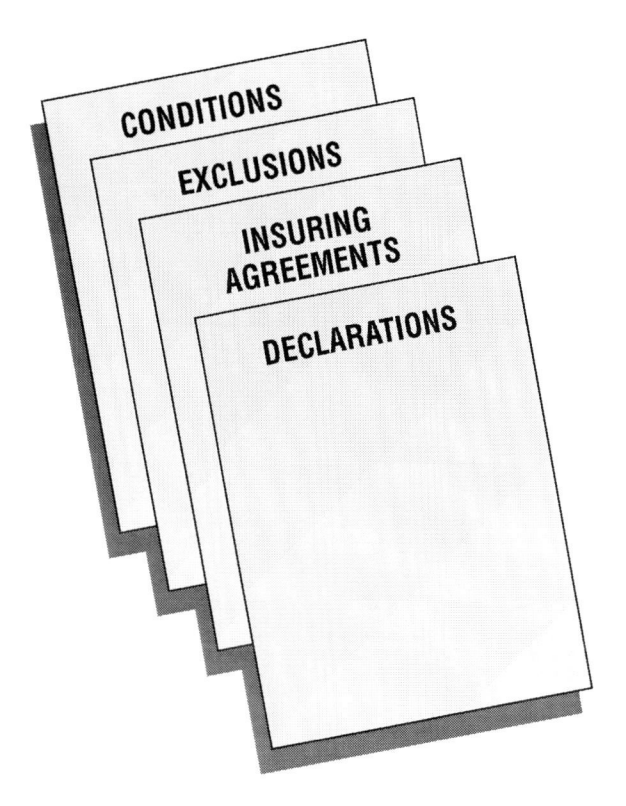

Name the four parts of an insurance policy.

A. _____

B. _____

C. _____

D. _____

Answer: Declarations, Insuring Agreements, Exclusions, Conditions (any order)

14. The **Declarations** section is almost always the first page of a policy. It contains, among other information, the name of the insured, the insured's address, the limit of indemnity or amount of insurance provided, the period during which coverage is in effect, and the cost of the policy. If it is a property policy, it will also contain a description of the insured property.

   The following examples are partial illustrations of each of a policy's four sections of a policy. At this point, we don't expect you to identify all four, but from what we have just covered, you should be able to pick out the Declarations section. Write the word "Declarations" beneath that part.

To pay on behalf of the insured all sums which the insured shall become legally obligated to pay as damages because of bodily injury, sickness, or disease arising out of the use of the owned automobile. A._____	When two or more automobiles are insured, the terms of the policy shall apply separately to each. B._____
Named Insured: Mr. John Doe Address: 5430 Overman Drive Description: 2-story frame house Property Class: HF Premium: $156 C._____	This policy does not apply to accidents caused directly or indirectly by hostile or warlike action. D._____

Answer: C. Declarations

15. The **Insuring Agreements section** contains the real substance of the policy. It tells the insured what types of losses are covered by the policy.

    Of the following, label those that are examples of either Insuring Agreements or Declarations.

The company's total liability for loss shall not exceed the specified limit per accident. A._____	Named Insured: Mr. James Watt Address: 1730 Brandenburg Property Description: Class 2 Boiler B._____
This policy does not apply to damage caused by the freezing of pipes. C._____	To pay for the reasonable cost of temporary repair or of expediting repair at a cost not to exceed $1,000. D._____

Answer: B. Declarations; D. Insuring Agreements

16. The **Exclusions section** describes the losses the policy does not cover. If an excluded loss occurs, the insurer will *not* indemnify the insured.

    Write the words "Exclusion," "Insuring Agreements," or "Declarations" under the appropriate parts of the policy.

The policy does not apply to loss caused by the ignition of escaping gas or bursting of pipes. A. _____	To defend the insured against any claim or suit as a result of the action of the insured. B. _____
The company shall be permitted at any time to inspect any object and the premises of the insured. C. _____	Named Insured: Mr. John Wolf Address: 6026 Century Drive Description of Property: Model 5 Widget Premium: $138 D. _____

Answer: A. Exclusions; B. Insuring Agreements; D. Declarations

17. The **Conditions section** states the "ground rules" for the policy. It describes the responsibilities of both the company and the insured.

    Write the words "Conditions," "Exclusions," "Insuring Agreements," or "Declarations" beneath the appropriate parts of the policy.

Named Insured: Mr. G. Washington Address: 1600 Pennsylvania Description of Property: House, white Premium: $379 A._____	When an accident occurs, written notice shall be given to the company within 24 hours. B._____
This policy does not apply to any act of insurrection, rebellion, revolution, or civil war. C._____	To pay for injury of others caused by the sudden and accidental dispersion of flying glass. D._____

    Answer: A. Declarations; B. Conditions; C. Exclusions; D. Insuring Agreements

Endorsements

18. Because everyone's circumstances are different, people often wish to make a change to a standard version of a policy. And because things change, existing policies sometimes need to be modified. For example, an insured may need to be added to a policy, or additional protection may be needed for certain property. Changes like these can be made by adding an **endorsement** to a policy.

    Which of the following are examples of endorsements?

    A. Mary Smith, now divorced and using her maiden name Jones, wants her automobile policy to reflect this change. The insurance company attaches a document to the policy indicating this change.

    B. The Kalamazoo Stove and Screen Door Company wants extra insurance coverage for the contents of a safe. The insurance company attaches a document to the policy to provide for this additional coverage.

    C. Bob Gold wishes to cancel his insurance. Upon receipt of the letter from Bob, his insurance company cancels his policy.

    Answer: A and B are correct.

Ask your supervisor for a sample copy of one of your company's policies and identify each of its sections.

Let's look now at the four main parts of an insurance policy in more detail.

DECLARATIONS

19. The first job of the Declarations section is to identify the named insured, whether it is an individual or a business. While others may be insured under a policy, it is the **named insured**, the individual or business named in the Declarations, who is responsible for paying premiums and reporting losses. Some policies have more than one named insured, as in the case of a husband and wife who are buying auto insurance.

    If it is a property insurance policy, the Declarations section also identifies the property being covered, whether it is a house at 1550 Willow, a 1996 Honda Accord, or a business premises.

    In an insurance policy, the named insured is

    A. anyone insured under the policy.
    B. the person or business identified in the Declarations.
    C. the insurance company.

    Answer: B is correct.

20. The Declarations also states the **policy period**, sometimes also called the **policy term**. The policy period begins on the policy's **effective date** (the time and date that coverage under the policy goes into effect) and it ends on the **expiration date** (the time and date that coverage under the policy expires).

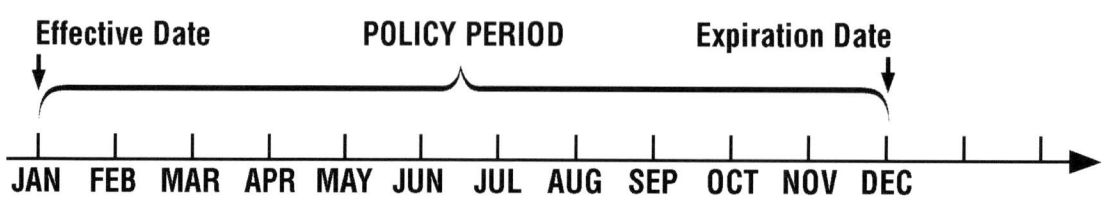

When Coverage Is in Effect

Effective Date → | POLICY PERIOD | ← Expiration Date

JAN FEB MAR APR MAY JUN JUL AUG SEP OCT NOV DEC

Many policies are **continuous**, ending on the expiration date only if the insured or the insurer chooses not to renew the policy.

The following dates appear on a policy: 1-1-99 to 1-1-00.
A. 1-1-99 is the policy's _____.
B. 1-1-00 is the policy's _____.
C. From 1-1-99 to 1-1-00 is called the _____.

Answer: A. effective date; B. expiration date; C. policy period or policy term

21. Another important piece of information contained in the Declarations is the **limit of insurance**. The limit of insurance represents the maximum dollar amount the insurance company will pay for a loss.

    The policy may have a **single limit** of insurance, or it may have **separate limits** of insurance applicable to each coverage provided under the policy.

    The limit of insurance is the
    A. flat amount the insured will collect for any loss.
    B. minimum amount the insured will collect for a loss.
    C. maximum amount the insured will collect for a loss.

    Answer: C is correct.

22. In property insurance, a single limit of insurance may apply to property at several different locations. This is known as **blanket insurance**. Other policies may feature a separate limit that applies to each location. This is known as **scheduled insurance**.
    A. A policy covers a manufacturer with several regional plants for up to $25,000 for any one loss, regardless of which plant incurs the loss. This is an example of (blanket/scheduled) _____ insurance.
    B. A policy covers a distributor with three different distribution points for up to the following amounts for a single loss: $15,000 for distribution point X, $10,000 for distribution point Y, and $5,000 for distribution point Z. This is an example of (blanket/scheduled) _____ insurance.

    Answer: A. blanket; B. scheduled

23. In liability insurance, the Declarations section may show, in addition to a limit of insurance, an **aggregate limit**. While the limit of insurance is the most the company will pay for any *one* loss, the aggregate limit is the maximum amount the insurer will pay for *all* losses under the policy during the policy term.

The Declarations page for a liability policy states that there is a $100,000 limit of insurance with a $300,000 aggregate limit.

A. If the insured suffers a single loss of $120,000, how much of that loss will the insurer pay? $_____

B. If the insured suffers three separate $100,000 losses, and then another $50,000 dollar loss, how much of the $50,000 loss will the insurer pay? $_____

Answer: A. $100,000 (this is the most the insurer will pay on any one loss); B. $0 (the aggregate limit under the policy has been reached).

Look at the sample policy you obtained from your supervisor to see what information it contains in its Declarations section.

INSURING AGREEMENT

Property Policies

Peril

24. The insuring agreement is the heart of the policy. It explains who is an insured, what property is covered, and under what circumstances.

    The insuring agreement of a property policy describes the perils insured against. As you'll recall, a peril is a cause of loss, such as fire, flood, or collision. Identify the perils described in the following examples.

    A. Harry's house burned down. The peril was _____.
    B. High water damaged Joan's house. The peril was _____.
    C. Sue hit Norman's car with hers. The peril was _____.

    Answer: A. fire; B. flood; C. collision

25. Ten perils commonly insured against under property insurance policies are: fire, explosion, wind, lightning, smoke, hail, aircraft, collision, riot, and theft. Many property policies also insure against damage caused by **vandalism and malicious mischief (V&MM)**. By working with these terms each day, you'll come to remember most of them.

For each of the following losses, write the name of the peril in the space provided.

A. A hot water heater relief valve failed to work. The resultant blast destroyed a self-service laundry in a trailer park. _____

B. In a traffic accident, an army tank hit a car, causing injury to the occupants of the car. _____

C. An employee, welding an overhead pipe, caused sparks to ignite a barrel of oil. The result was $5,000,000 damage to property. _____

D. During a severe storm, a TV antenna on top of a house was struck by an electrical discharge from a cloud, causing substantial damage to the wiring of the house. _____

E. Two planes collided over a residential area. One fell on a home, destroying it. _____

F. A manufacturer experienced considerable damage to a building when a crowd of striking workers began smashing windows and throwing bricks. _____

G. An electrical fire in a computer center was confined to a small area, but the thick vapors from burning insulation caused damage to a large number of sensitive computer components. _____

H. A safe containing $17,000 in cash was taken from a warehouse. _____

I. A tornado destroyed several neighborhoods, causing over $15 million in damage. _____

J. A spring storm rained ice pellets the size of nickels on a community, damaging thousands of cars that were parked outside. _____

K. Two teenagers with a baseball broke several car windows in an isolated parking lot. _____

Answer: A. Explosion; B. Collision; C. Fire; D. Lightning; E. Aircraft; F. Riot; G. Smoke; H. Theft; I. Wind; J. Hail; K. Vandalism and malicious mischief

26. Some property insurance policies list the specific perils insured against. These are called **specified peril** or **named peril** policies. These policies insure property only against the causes of loss, or perils, that are listed.

Specified Perils Versus Open Perils

We insure for loss caused by:	We insure against risk of loss EXCEPT FOR:
• _____	• _____
• _____	• _____
• _____	• _____
• _____	• _____
• _____	• _____
• _____	• _____
• _____	• _____
• _____	• _____
SPECIFIED PERIL	**OPEN PERILS**

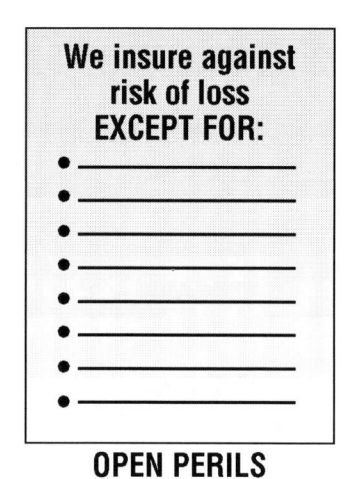

Some property insurance policies do not list specific perils, but instead insure against perils not specifically excluded. These are called **open perils** or **special coverage** policies. They are also sometimes referred to as **all risk** policies, but many companies avoid this term because no policy actually covers *all* risks of loss. Under these types of policies, risks not otherwise excluded are covered.

Identify the following Insuring Agreements as being from a specified peril or an open peril policy.

A. "This policy insures against loss or damage to goods caused by fire, lightning, self-ignition, and internal explosion."
( ) Specified peril   ( ) Open peril

B. "This policy insures against risks of direct physical loss of or damage to the insured property except as specifically excluded."
( ) Specified peril   ( ) Open peril

Answer: A. Specified peril; B. Open peril

Direct Loss, Indirect Loss

27. In addition to identifying the property covered and the perils insured against, a property policy will state whether it covers **direct loss**, **indirect loss**, or both.

    You are probably most familiar with direct loss. This is financial loss that results directly from a loss to property, such as a house being damaged in a windstorm or a valuable piece of jewelry being stolen.

    Indirect loss comes as a result of the direct loss. Since it arises as a consequence of the direct loss, it is also known as **consequential loss**.

    For example, suppose a hotel burns to the ground. The cost to rebuild the hotel is $1 million. That's the direct loss. In the six months it takes to rebuild the hotel, it could have earned $200,000 in room rent if it hadn't burned. That's the indirect loss. If it takes a year to rebuild the hotel, the indirect loss will be $400,000. Because time plays such an important role in determining the extent of an indirect loss, coverage for these losses is often called **time element coverage**.

Identify the following losses as being direct or indirect.

A. After an explosion on its premises, a business has to rent space in another building during the period its own building is being repaired. _____

B. Thieves rob a bank, absconding with $4,000 cash. _____

C. A family has to pay to live in a hotel while its home is rebuilt after a fire. _____

Answer: A. Indirect; B. Direct; C. Indirect

Liability Policies

28. So far we've talked about the Insuring Agreements section of property policies. The Insuring Agreements section of liability policies is different in that it does not cover property against various perils. Most liability policies agree to pay, on behalf of the insured, amounts the insured becomes legally liable to pay as damages because of **bodily injury (BI)** or **property damage (PD)**.

    Bodily injury can include injury, sickness, or death. Property damage means damage to or destruction of property. Remember that a liability policy does not reimburse an insured for injury or damage to property, but rather reimburses insureds for their liability (or legal responsibility) for injuring others or damaging their property.

    Business liability insurance policies often include coverage for **personal injury** and **advertising injury**. Personal injury usually means injury other than bodily injury that arises out of such things as **slander** (making false and damaging remarks about another person), **libel** (writing something that wrongly gives a bad impression of another person), **invasion of privacy**, or other violations of a person's rights. Advertising injury includes such things as copyright infringement or stealing advertising ideas.

    Identify each of the following liability losses by writing "bodily injury," "property damage," "personal injury," or "advertising injury" in the blank provided.

    A. A truck driven by Bart veers off the road and jackknifes, killing 70 head of cattle he was transporting. _____

    B. John repeats rumors, not knowing whether or not they are true, about defects in a competitor's product in order to increase sales of his own product. _____

    C. Garret hits Cheri's car when he runs a red light. Cheri ends up with whiplash. _____

    D. Dierdre, using an existing advertisement for inspiration, creates a new ad for a customer with much of the same wording as the original. _____

Answer: A. Property damage; B. Personal injury; C. Bodily injury; D. Advertising injury

> *Look at the sample policy you obtained from your supervisor, and read the Insuring Agreement.*

EXCLUSIONS

29. Exclusions in a policy vary depending on the type of coverage (property or liability) and the situations the contract is designed to cover. But every insurance contract has exclusions. Even specified peril property insurance policies, which automatically exclude any perils not specifically mentioned, list certain exclusions separately to explain or emphasize perils or property excluded from coverage. Let's look at five broad types of exclusions that insurance policies commonly contain.

- ■ *Nonaccidental Losses*. Nonaccidental losses are excluded, since they are not risks, but certainties. Wear and tear, deterioration, rust, and corrosion are all examples of nonaccidental losses excluded from property insurance policies. "Inherent vice" is another example of nonaccidental loss. It refers to a condition or defect that exists in a product naturally. For example, rubber tends to deteriorate with age. This is inherent vice and would not be covered under an insurance contract. Liability policies exclude coverage of liability for damage caused intentionally by the insured since this would be a nonaccidental loss.

- ■ *Losses Controllable by the Insured*. Losses that the insured can control or prevent with some effort or care are excluded. This encourages insureds to be responsible in their actions. Marring, scratching, breaking, or chipping of fragile objects, illegal acts of the insured, and errors in workmanship are all examples of losses that insureds can control.

- ■ *Extra-Hazardous Risks*. Certain risks are extra-hazardous. The insurance company could provide coverage, but the unique nature of the risk would mean the insured would have to pay a much bigger premium. Policies usually exclude extra-hazardous risks since many insureds would not want or need the coverage. Those insureds who need the coverage can often obtain it through an endorsement to the policy, in return for an extra premium.

- ■ *Catastrophic Losses*. Some losses are so widespread that they could bankrupt any company that insured against them. Losses caused by war or nuclear peril are generally uninsurable because they are catastrophic.

- ■ *Risks Covered by Other Policies*. Risks that are covered by other insurance policies are excluded. For instance, a policy covering your personal property would normally exclude your car since there is a separate auto policy to provide coverage for your vehicles. Liability policies contain a similar exclusion, for the same reason.

Ready to review? Column A, following, lists perils or property often excluded. Column B lists the five major categories of exclusions. Match each exclusion in Column A with the category in Column B.

Column A

____ A. Wear and tear
____ B. Scratching
____ C. Earthquake
____ D. Dishonesty of the insured
____ E. Nuclear peril
____ F. Automobile

Column B

1. Nonaccidental loss
2. Losses controllable by the insured
3. Catastrophic losses
4. Extra-hazardous risks
5. Property covered in other policies

Answer: 1 A.; 2 B.; 4 C.; 2 D.; 3 E.; 5 F.

Look at the sample policy you obtained from your supervisor to see what Exclusions it contains.

CONDITIONS

Cancellation

30. The **Conditions** section of the insurance policy defines terms and lists the responsibilities and privileges of both the insured and the insurer. The first condition we'll look at is the **Cancellation condition**.

    At times, the insured or the insurance company may wish to cancel the insurance before the policy expires. The Cancellation condition states the circumstances under which a policy can be canceled.

Cancellation

INSURER CANCELS — Advance Notice Required

INSURED CANCELS — Effective Immediately

ABC INSURANCE COMPANY

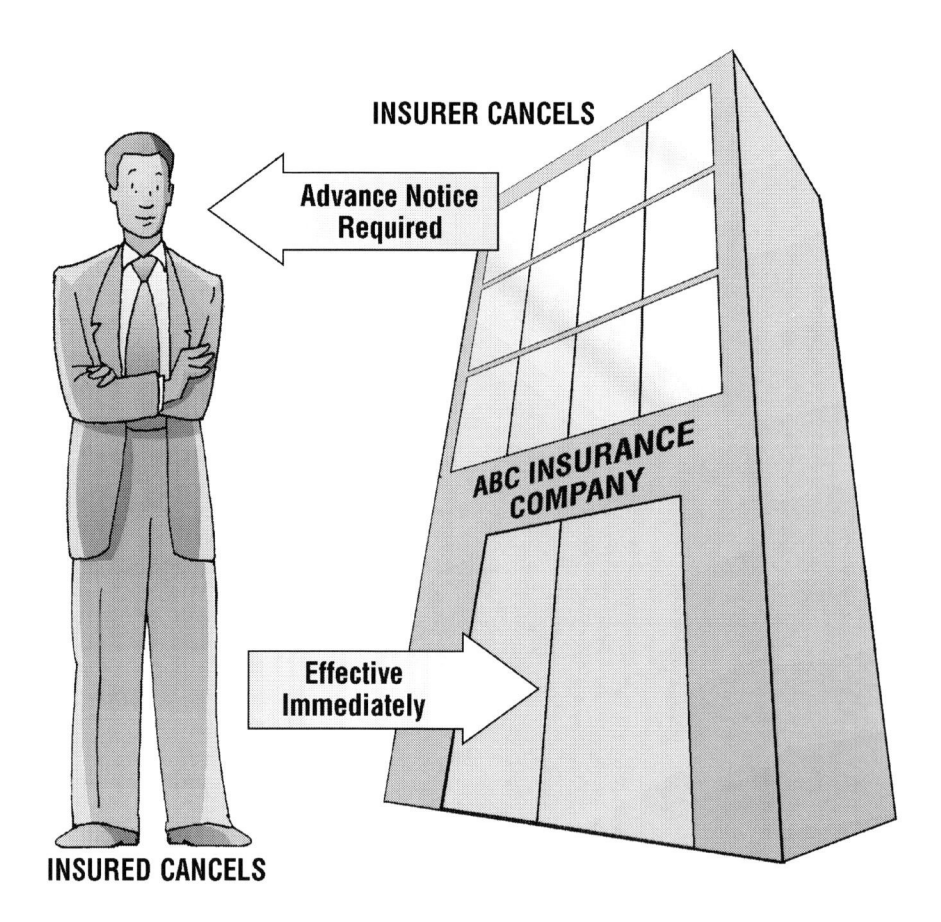

The insured may cancel the policy at any time by writing a letter to the insurance company or by surrendering the policy to the company.

The insurance company does not have the same freedom to cancel that the insured does. Each state has rules that restrict an insurer's right to cancel a policy.

Most states do not allow insurers to cancel unless they have a good reason, such as nonpayment of premium. When the company does cancel, state laws and policy terms require the company to notify the insured in advance and in writing, usually within a specified period of time such as 5 or 10 days.

When an insurer cancels a policy, it must return the unearned part of the premium to the insured. Many policies state that the insurer will make a **pro rata** premium refund on a canceled policy, meaning that the premium returned will be in proportion to the unexpired term of the policy. For example, if Bob's policy is canceled halfway through the policy term, he'll get half his premium back.

Some policies call for pro rata cancellation when the insurance company cancels the policy and **short-rate** cancellation when the insured cancels the policy. A short-rate premium refund means that the insurance company will keep not only the amount of premium earned up to the cancellation date, but also an additional amount to cover some of its expenses of issuing the policy.

When a policy is canceled before its effective date by either the insured or the insurance company, the entire premium is returned to the policyholder. This is called **flat cancellation**.

Indicate whether each of the following statements concerning cancellation is true or false.
A. The insurance company has the right to cancel a policy for any reason.   ( ) True   ( ) False
B. When the insured cancels the policy, he or she must notify the company in writing or surrender the policy.   ( ) True   ( ) False
C. When the insurance company cancels a policy, it refunds unearned premium on a short-rate basis.   ( ) True   ( ) False
D. Flat cancellation occurs whenever the insured cancels the policy.   ( ) True   ( ) False

Answer: A. False; B. True; C. False; D. False

31. When a policy reaches its expiration date, the company will usually renew it for another term, as long as both the insured and the insurer want the coverage to continue.
    Of course, the insured has the option not to renew the insurance at this point. The insurance company may also decide not to renew the policy. Although **nonrenewal** provisions are usually less restrictive than those for cancellation, the law may still limit the reasons that insurance companies may nonrenew, and it may specify the type of nonrenewal notice insurers must give to insureds.

    It's April 1, and Ben's policy with XYZ Insurance Company expires on June 1. XYZ does not wish to continue insuring Ben, so it sends him a notice stating that coverage will not continue beyond June 1. This is an example of a
    A. cancellation.
    B. nonrenewal.
    C. suspension.
    D. binder.

    Answer: B is correct.

Misrepresentation, Concealment, Fraud

32. As we just mentioned, insurers may cancel an insurance policy only under specific circumstances. State statutes as well as the policy spell out these circumstances. Nonpayment of premium is one. Others are **misrepresentation, concealment,** and **fraud**.
    Misrepresentation is stating something that is untrue. Concealment means withholding facts that should be given to the insurer. Fraud is a false statement that is intended to deceive the insurer and make it give up a legal right or something of value. An example of fraud would be reporting a loss that never occurred in order to collect payment on the claim.

Fraud generally voids a policy, but the same is not true of all misrepresentation or concealment. The misrepresentation or concealment must be intentional, and it must concern a **material fact**. A material fact is a fact that, if the company had known it, would have made the company decline the risk, charge a higher premium, or include different provisions than those that were included.

Consider the case of Lyle E. Taylor, who wants to insure his home with ABC Insurance Company. Mr. Taylor hates his middle name "Elwood," so he doesn't give the insurance company his middle name.

A. This is (misrepresentation/concealment) _____ .

B. Is it intentional?   ( ) Yes   ( ) No

C. Would his action void the policy?   ( ) Yes   ( ) No

D. Suppose Mr. Taylor told ABC Insurance Company that he used his home solely as a residence, when actually he used it as an ammunition warehouse. This is (misrepresentation/concealment) _____ _____ .

E. Do you think this could be grounds for voiding the contract?
( ) Yes   ( ) No

Answer: A. concealment; B. Yes; C. No (it did not concern a material fact); D. misrepresentation; E. Yes (it was intentional and concerned a material fact).

Representations and Warranties

33. Most of the statements contained in the insured's application for insurance are **representations**—statements the applicant believes to be true.

    Sometimes, though, insurers require insureds to meet some specific conditions. These agreements become a part of the policy. For example, let's say that as a condition of insuring Helen's business, XYZ requires Helen to have a watchperson on duty whenever the business is closed. This agreement is called a **warranty**.

    As long as Helen keeps the agreement, the warranty is valid, and the insurer provides insurance protection. If Helen doesn't keep a watchperson on duty when the business is closed, XYZ can suspend the policy. A suspension is a temporary situation that occurs when an insured fails to live up to a warranty. Once the violation is corrected, the suspension can be lifted.

    Suppose Helen also warranted that she would maintain heat in the building as a condition of obtaining coverage from XYZ against damage caused by freezing and bursting pipes. An inspector from XYZ discovers that there is no heat in the building. What would XYZ probably do?

Answer: Suspend the policy

Assignment

34. Property insurance protecting a building is often transferred—or **assigned**—to a new property owner if a building is sold. The **Assignment condition** states that a policy may only be assigned with the insurance company's consent.

    Can you think why an insurance company would want to know who is moving into a building upon which it has insurance? _____

    Answer: To determine possible moral, morale, or physical hazards

Duties Following Loss

35. Most policies include a **Duties Following Loss** clause that describes what insureds must do when a loss occurs. For property insurance policies, insureds generally must: notify the company in writing that a loss has occurred, protect the property from further damage, complete a detailed proof of loss (an official inventory of the damages), make the property available to the company for inspection, and allow the company to examine them under oath if it wishes. Liability policies require insureds to forward to the insurance company any documents they receive as part of a liability suit. Liability insurers also forbid the insured to voluntarily assume any liability without the insurance company's consent.

    Which of the following would typically be included as duties the insured has if a loss occurs? (Check all that apply.)
    A. Make the property available for inspection
    B. Notify the insurance company of the loss in writing
    C. Submit the policy to the insurance company
    D. Complete a proof of loss

    Answer: A, B, and D are correct.

Valuation

36. Determining the right amount to pay insureds takes a big part of the time spent handling claims. The **Valuation condition** states how the insurer will determine the amount of a property loss and how it will reimburse the insured.

    One term commonly used in determining indemnification in property losses is **Actual Cash Value (ACV)**. Insurance companies commonly use this formula for determining ACV.

ACV Formula

REPLACEMENT COST *MINUS* **DEPRECIATION** *EQUALS* **ACTUAL CASH VALUE**

A. Marjorie paid $3,500 for new dining room furniture. It had depreciated a total of $1,400 before an explosion destroyed it. Marjorie learns that it will cost $5,000 to replace this furniture. What is its ACV? $_____

B. A fire destroys Bill's eight-year-old washing machine. He paid $650 for it when it was new. It depreciated $200 the first year he owned it, $150 the second year and $20 each of the remaining six. A new machine will cost him $800. What is the ACV of the washing machine that was destroyed? $_____

Answer: A. $3,600 (replacement cost of $5,000 minus $1,400 of depreciation) B. $330 (replacement cost of $800, minus $470 total depreciation)

37. The reason that depreciation is figured into ACV calculations is that the insured has had the use of the item for some period of time. To indemnify the full replacement cost might lead to the insured making a profit on the loss of the property. Making a profit on a loss would violate the principle of indemnity.

However, some policies will pay for certain losses on a **replacement cost** basis rather than ACV, and the insured may have the option of buying replacement cost coverage. Replacement Cost coverage pays for losses with no deduction for depreciation.

Some policies pay for losses based on **market value**—what the property could have been sold for at the time of the loss. Market value can differ from replacement cost. For example, suppose Ed spends $400,000 to build a fancy house in an open area, but then the land around it is zoned for heavy industry and a bad-smelling oil refinery is built nearby. Because Ed might have trouble finding a buyer, his house may only have a market value of $250,000 in that location, even though it would still cost about $400,000 to rebuild it if it were destroyed.

Note that in auto insurance losses, the car's actual cash value is its market value at the time of the loss. The car's age, mileage and overall condition are among the factors considered in determining market value.

Go through the following examples, identifying each one as Actual Cash Value (ACV), replacement cost (RC), or market value (MV).

_____ A. A two-year-old auto is stolen. The insurance company pays an amount equal to the value of a similar used auto.

_____ B. A fire partially destroys the roof of a 40-year-old house. The insurance company pays for the entire amount of the roof to be replaced.

_____ C. The insured had a two-year-old electric stove destroyed when lightning struck the wires going into the house. The insurance company provides the insured with a new stove.

_____ D. An explosion destroys an aging factory. The insurance company pays the insured the amount that a buyer would have been willing to pay for the factory just before the explosion occurred.

_____ E. A fire breaks out in the insured's home. The insurance company pays only $10,000 for damages after deducting an amount equal to 10 years of depreciation.

Answer: ACV A.; RC B.; RC C.; MV D.; ACV E.

Coinsurance

38. Another very important loss condition featured by some property insurance policies is a **Coinsurance condition**. This condition states the minimum amount of insurance the insured should carry on the covered property. The policy states this coinsurance requirement as a certain percentage of the property's value. For instance, a policy with an 80% coinsurance clause requires an insured to insure the property for at least 80% of its value.

    Let's see how the Coinsurance condition works. Suppose property is valued at $40,000. With an 80% coinsurance clause, the insured will be required to carry at least $32,000 of coverage ($40,000 × 80%).

    Now you try a few. We'll give you the coinsurance percentage and the value of the property. You fill in the minimum amount of insurance needed to fulfill the coinsurance requirement. We've done the first one for you.

Coinsurance Percentage	Property Value	Required Amount of Insurance
80%	$60,000	$48,000
90%	$10,000	A. _____
80%	$20,000	B. _____
60%	$100,000	C. _____

Answer: A. $9,000; B. $16,000; C. $60,000

39. As long as an insured carries insurance equal to at least the value required by the coinsurance clause, the insurance company will indemnify losses up to the limits of the policy.

    For example, suppose Don has a building valued at $70,000. The insurance policy Don buys for the property has an 80% coinsurance clause, so Don should carry at least $56,000 of coverage. If Don carries $60,000 of insurance and the building is totally destroyed, the insurance company will pay Don $60,000—the full amount of the loss up to the policy limits.

    But what if Don didn't meet the coinsurance requirements? Suppose he carried only $50,000 of coverage. In that case, a penalty would be applied. The insurance company would not reimburse Don up to the policy limits, even though the loss exceeded that amount. In effect, Don would become a coinsurer with the insurance company.

    An insured has property valued at $50,000 that she insures for $30,000. The policy contains an 80% coinsurance clause.

    A. How much insurance should the insured carry? _____
    B. Does the insured meet the coinsurance requirement?   ( ) Yes   ( ) No
    C. How will this affect the insured's reimbursement for the loss, in general? _____
    _____

    Answer: A. $40,000 ($50,000 x 80%); B. No; C. The insured will not be reimbursed by the company up to the policy limits.

40. The formula for determining how much the insurance company will pay on a loss when the insured fails to meet the coinsurance requirement is a simple one.

    $$\frac{\text{Amount Carried}}{\text{Amount Required}} \times \text{Amount of Loss} = \text{Maximum Amount of Recovery}$$

    Let's work one together.

    Let's say Jack has property valued at $70,000. He has it insured under a policy with an 80% coinsurance requirement. Jack carries $28,000 of insurance and suffers a $20,000 loss. How much will Jack collect for this loss?

    The first step is to determine whether or not Jack has met the coinsurance requirement. $70,000 times 80% is $56,000. Jack carries only $28,000, and so he does not meet the coinsurance requirement.

    To determine how much he will be reimbursed for the loss, we divide the amount of coverage he carried by the amount he was supposed to carry and then multiply it by the amount of the loss:

    $$\frac{\$28,000 \text{ (amount carried)}}{\$56,000 \text{ (amount required)}} \times \$20,000 = \text{recovery}$$

    $28,000 divided by $56,000 is one-half. One-half of $20,000 is $10,000. Therefore, the insurer will pay Jack $10,000 on this loss.

    Now you try one.

Value of property: $100,000
Coinsurance required: 80%
Amount of coverage carried: $40,000
Amount of loss: $6,000

A. The amount of coverage that should be carried is
$ _____.

B. The amount carried divided by the amount required is
$ _____.

C. So the amount of recovery is $ _____.

Answer: A. $80,000 ($100,000 x 80%); B. one-half ($40,000/$80,000); C. $3,000 (one-half of $6,000)

41. Coinsurance serves a very important function. In most cases, property is not totally destroyed, but only damaged. For this reason, policyholders may be tempted to insure property for only part of its value, and thus save part of the premium. If insurers allowed that, insureds would not have adequate coverage when large or total losses occurred. What is more, insurance companies would not have enough funds accumulated to pay for covered losses.

    In addition, by agreeing to keep the insurance to the value required by the policy, insureds receive a premium reduction. The coinsurance clause applies a penalty only if the insured doesn't keep that agreement.

    In your own words, explain why insurers require policyholders to insure property to value. _____

    Answer: So that the insured will have coverage for large losses, and so that the company will have accumulated adequate funds to pay for losses

Deductible

42. To reduce the cost of insurance, companies use a **deductible** amount, which means that the insured pays the first dollar amount of any loss, up to the amount of the deductible. The amount of the deductible is stated in the Declarations.

How Deductibles Work

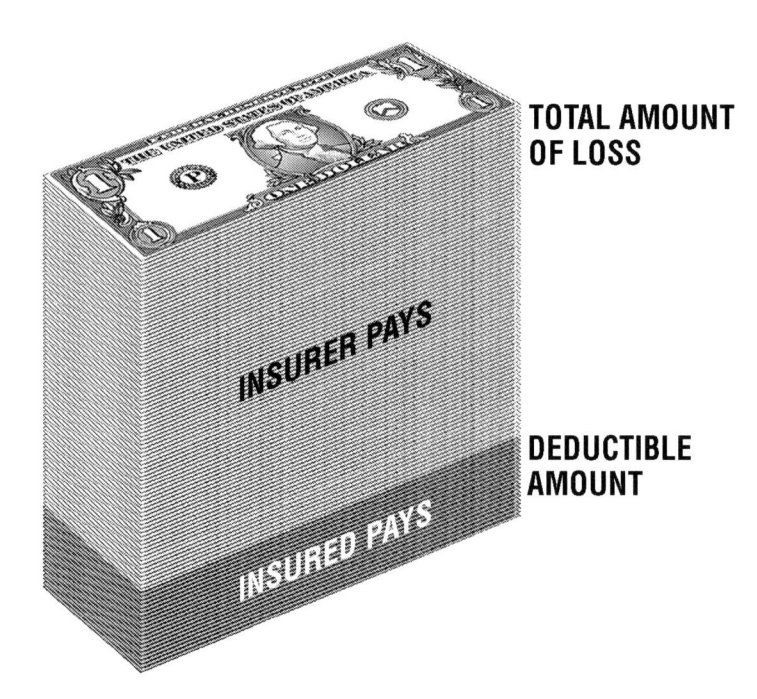

Mr. Shelby has insurance protection for his home with a $200 deductible clause. One night, a severe windstorm tears off part of the roof. The loss is $500.

A. How much will the insured pay? _____
B. How much will the company pay? _____

Answer: A. $200; B. $300

Mortgage or Loss Payable Clause

43. Earlier in this course, we talked about the subject of joint insurable interest. Whenever people borrow money to pay for property, the lender has an interest in the property—an insurable interest. When the loan is secured by a mortgage, the lender is the **mortgagee**. For other types of loans, the lender may be referred to as the **loss payee**.

    The **Mortgage** or **Loss Payable condition** entitles the lender to collect for a loss under the policy up to its financial interest in the property.

    Suppose Bill buys a house with $100,000 borrowed from the Last American Bank. Bill has paid back only $5,000 so far. At this point, what is the amount of the Last American Bank's financial interest in Bill's house?
    $_____

Answer: $95,000

Subrogation

44. Another clause found in many policies is the **Subrogation condition**. Subrogation means that someone transfers his or her lawful claim to another

person or company. It works like this: suppose Dave's auto hits yours in the rear. Result—$400 damage to your car. Unfortunately, Dave has no insurance. The coverage you carry for collisions has a $250 deductible. Your company will pay for your collision, even though Dave was at fault.

A. How much does your company pay you? _____

B. How much must you pay? _____

Answer: A. $150—the amount in excess of the deductible; B. $250—the deductible amount

45. Your company has now paid part of the loss. You have paid part of the loss. And the accident was not your fault! Your company will now try to collect from Dave and possibly bring suit against him on your behalf as well as in its own behalf to collect the money that was paid. Your right to collect has been transferred, in part, to your insurance company. This transfer to the company of your right to collect is called subrogation. An insurance company may subrogate against an individual third party or against the third party's insurance company.

Which of the following is an example of subrogation?

A. Harvey runs off the road and damages his car, resulting in $650 of damage. He pays the first $100, and his insurance company pays the rest.

B. Edgar and Lorna's cars collide at an intersection. Edgar is determined to be at fault. Edgar's insurance company pays for damages to Lorna's car.

C. Pete is seriously injured in an auto accident that he says was Dierdre's fault, but Dierdre's insurance company doesn't want to pay. Pete's insurance company pays for his hospital bills, then goes to court to begin collection of the amount from Dierdre's insurance company.

Answer: C is correct.

Other Insurance

46. Some insureds have been known to buy identical insurance from two or more companies.

Suppose Betty has two $45,000 policies covering her house. Her home is valued at $45,000. To receive $90,000 in the event her house burned down would violate the principle of indemnity.

To prevent this "double payment," most policies contain an **Other Insurance condition** that describes how such situations will be handled. Some policies prohibit other insurance on the same interest without the consent of the company. Other policies say that when other insurance exists, they will pay only any excess beyond what any other policy pays. So if Company Y's policy would cover $10,000 of a $15,000 loss, Company X would pay no more than $5,000.

But the most common method is **apportionment**, or the "pro rata" method, in which a company agrees to pay only a proportion of any loss that is also covered by another policy. For instance, if the insured carried 30% of the total insurance coverage on her house with Company X, Company X would pay no more than 30% of a loss to which other insurance also applied.

With a policy containing an apportionment clause, how much would two companies pay for an $80,000 loss if each had the same proportion of the insurance coverage? _____

Answer: $40,000

Appraisal and Arbitration

47. Sometimes an insured and an insurer cannot agree on the amount of a loss. The **Appraisal condition** of a property insurance contract says that both parties can obtain the service of an appraiser. If the appraisers cannot agree on an amount, then they submit their differences to an **umpire**. The decision agreed to by any two of the three is the final amount of indemnification.

    An **Arbitration condition** is similar, but arbitration is not limited to disagreements about the value of a loss. It may also be used when other types of disagreements arise between an insured and an insurance company, between a company and a third party in the case of liability insurance, or between two insurers.

    Suppose Kyle owned an antique organ that a fire destroyed. Kyle's insurance company says it will pay him $350. Kyle feels the organ was worth at least $600. Two appraisers are called in. One calculates the loss at $250, the other at $550. When they finally call in an umpire, the umpire agrees that reimbursement should be for $550. How much would Kyle be paid?

    A. $350
    B. $550
    C. $600
    D. $250

    Answer: B is correct.

Look at the sample policy you obtained from your supervisor to see what conditions it contains.

You now have an idea of the structure of the insurance contract in general and the kinds of information included in a policy. In the next unit, we'll look at the variety of coverages offered by a number of specific property-casualty insurance policies.

UNIT 6

Property-Casualty Insurance Policies

1. You've learned that there are two major groups of property-casualty insurance policies: personal policies that insure individuals and families and commercial policies that insure businesses. In this unit, you'll become acquainted with major policies that make up these two broad categories of insurance. Note that our discussion focuses on the standard policies issued by the Insurance Services Office (ISO).

PERSONAL LINES POLICIES

Homeowners Policies

2. If you are a homeowner, condominium owner or the renter of a home, apartment or condominium, you've made a sizable investment in that dwelling and/or the personal property in it. But, unfortunately, in making that investment, you have exposed yourself to risk of financial loss from unpredictable events. For example, there is the risk your dwelling and/or all the personal property in it could be destroyed and need to be replaced, or it could be extensively damaged and need major and costly repairs. You also face the risk of someone stealing the personal property in your dwelling. And there is always a risk of an accident occurring on your property for which you could be held legally liable. In that case, a court might order you to pay damages because someone was injured or their property was damaged in the accident.

    You can protect yourself against exposure to such risks by insuring your property and your legal liability. One way to do this is with a **homeowners policy**.

    There are six separate homeowners policies that provide varying levels of coverage for homeowners and specialized coverages for renters or condominium owners. To qualify for a homeowners policy, you must own and reside in your insured home or condominium or rent or reside in the apartment or condominium that contains your personal property.

    A. If you and your family occupy the home you own, could you insure it under a homeowners policy?   ( ) Yes   ( ) No

    B. If you rent an apartment, could you insure your personal property that's in that apartment under a homeowners policy?   ( ) Yes   ( ) No

    C. If you own a two-unit apartment home, but live in another home, could you insure the apartment home under a homeowners policy?
    ( ) Yes   ( ) No

    Answer: A. Yes; B. Yes; C. No

Homeowners Section I Coverages

3. The homeowners forms are divided into two main sections. The coverages in **Section I** cover the insured's property.

Homeowners Section I—Property Coverages

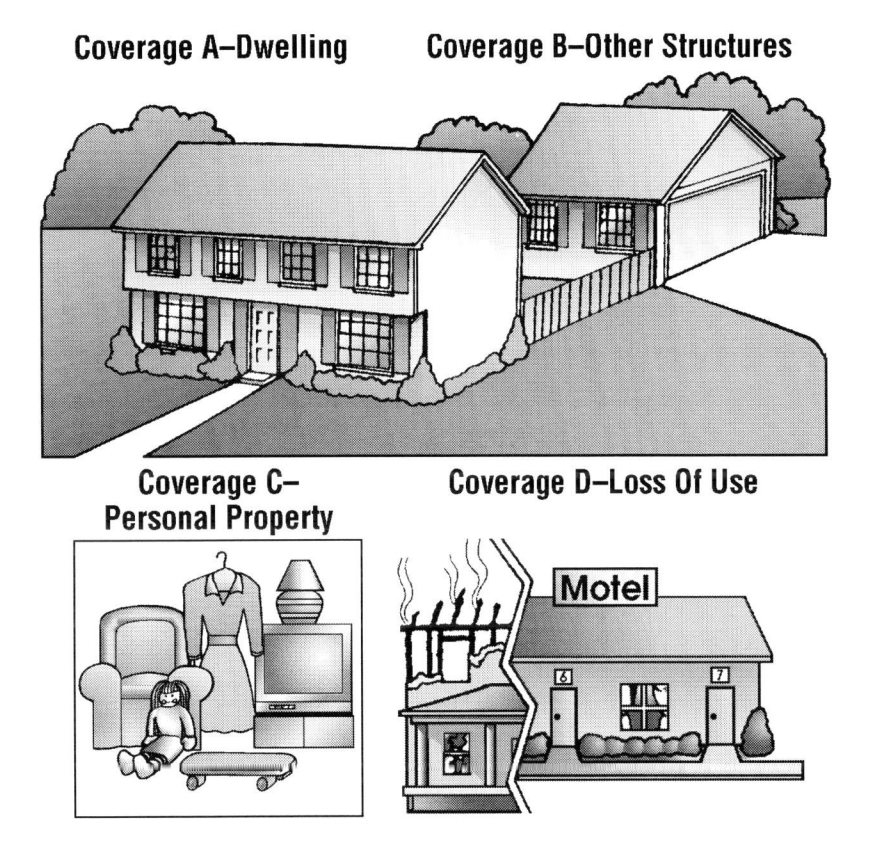

Coverage A—Dwelling

Coverage B—Other Structures

Coverage C—Personal Property

Coverage D—Loss Of Use

    Coverage A—Dwelling provides insurance protection for your dwelling and structures attached to your dwelling.
    Coverage B—Other Structures covers other structures on your premises, such as a detached garage or minibarn.
    Coverage C—Personal Property covers the contents of your dwelling, such as furniture, appliances, clothing and toys.
    Coverage D—Loss Of Use covers loss of rents if you are temporarily unable to rent a portion of the dwelling that you rent out to others. It also provides coverage if you have to vacate your insured premises due to covered damage and pays when you have to stay in a hotel or an apartment until the damage can be repaired. This is often referred to as **time element** coverage.

Which of the following might be covered under Section I of a homeowners policy?

A. Your house

B. A storage shed on your property

C. Your sofa

D. Extra expense you incur to stay in a hotel while your home is being repaired after it is damaged in a fire

Answer: All are correct.

Perils Covered in Homeowners Policies

4. The homeowners forms insure against a list of named or specified perils or against all risks of direct physical loss except as specifically excluded by the policy. The latter is usually known as "open perils" coverage and is sometimes also called "all risk" coverage.

    Homeowners 2 Broad form will insure your dwelling, other structures and personal property against a limited list of perils.

    Homeowners 3 Special form provides open perils rather than named perils coverage for the dwelling and other structures and named perils coverage for personal property.

    Homeowners 4 Contents Broad form for renters insures only personal property against the same perils as the Homeowners 2.

    Homeowners 5 Comprehensive form provides open peril coverage for both buildings and personal property.

    Homeowners 6 Unit-Owners form for owners of condominium units insures against the same perils as the Homeowners 2. While it primarily covers personal property, it also provides limited coverage for items the insured owns or is responsible for insuring, such as alterations and improvements to the dwelling or other structures made by the insured, and appliances and fixtures.

    Homeowners 8 Modified Coverage form insures buildings and personal property against a basic list of perils.

    Following is a summary of which homeowners forms provide basic, broad or special property coverage and for which types of property:

Homeowners Property Coverages

	HO 00 02	HO 00 03	HO 00 04	HO 00 05	HO 00 06	HO 00 08
Special Coverage		Dwelling		Dwelling & Personal Property		
Broad Coverage	Dwelling & Personal Property	Personal Property	Personal Property		Personal Property	
Basic Coverage						Dwelling & Personal Property

Key: ■ = Dwelling ▫ = Personal Property

A. A homeowners policy states that it insures against loss or damage to insured property caused by fire, lightning, windstorm, explosion, and theft. This is (an open/a specified) _____ perils policy.

B. A homeowners policy states that it insures against risks of direct physical loss of or damage to insured property except as specifically excluded. This is (an open/a specified) _____ perils policy.

Answer: A. a specified; B. an open

Homeowners Section II Coverages

5. **Section II** of the homeowners policy provides liability and medical payments coverage.

    Coverage E—Personal Liability provides coverage when you are legally liable to pay because of bodily injury or property damage that arose out of your or your family's personal, nonbusiness activities or from your insured premises. For example, your liability would be covered if a guest was injured while on your property or if you accidentally injured someone's eye with an umbrella while boarding a bus.

    Coverage E– Personal Liability

    Coverage F– Medical Payments To Others

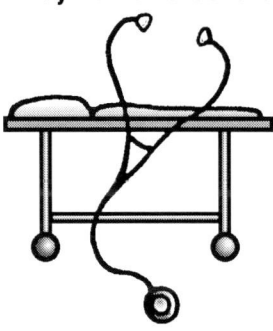

    In addition, the policy promises to defend you against lawsuits and pay other miscellaneous claim and lawsuit expenses, such as expenses you might incur at the insurance company's request, or your loss of earnings (up to a specified amount) because of time you had to take off work to assist in investigating the claim or defending a suit.

    Coverage F—Medical Payments To Others covers medical bills (up to a specified amount) incurred by people who are injured on your property or as a result of your personal activities. It pays whether or not you are legally at fault.

Which of the following might be covered under Section II of a homeowners policy?

A. Your dog bit a neighbor. The neighbor had $350 in medical bills.

B. Your home is damaged by lightning.

C. A woman delivering a package slipped on ice on your porch and broke a leg. The woman expects you to pay the medical bills for her injuries as well as the wages she will lose because she cannot work until her leg heals.

D. Assume you are flying a radio-controlled airplane from the backyard of your home. The plane damages guttering on a neighbor's house. The neighbor expects you to pay the $200 it will cost to repair the guttering.

Answer: A, C and D are correct.

Dwelling Policies

6. You'll recall that to qualify for a *homeowners policy*, you must own and reside in your insured home or condominium or rent and reside in the apartment or condominium that contains your insured personal property. You can also insure this dwelling under a **dwelling policy**. But, if you own a home you *don't* live in, you must insure it under a dwelling policy.

    There are three separate dwelling policies that, like the homeowners policies, range in coverage from basic to special:

    - DP-1 Basic form
    - DP-2 Broad form
    - DP-3 Special form

    While the dwelling forms themselves provide only coverage for your dwelling and personal property, you can add Liability and Theft coverages by endorsement.

    A. If you and your family occupy the home you own, could you insure it under a dwelling policy?   ( ) Yes   ( ) No

    B. If you own a two-family dwelling but live in another home, could you insure the two-family dwelling under a dwelling policy?   ( ) Yes   ( ) No

    Answer: A. Yes; B. Yes

Personal Auto Policy

7. Homeowners and dwelling policies exclude coverage to autos and legal liability associated with owning and using cars and other vehicles. Your family car is considered a specialized risk, and you can only insure it under a separate policy, the **Personal Auto policy (PAP)**, designed specifically for this purpose.

The PAP will provide broad coverage for your auto exposures under its four coverage parts:

- Part A—Liability Coverage
- Part B—Medical Payments Coverage
- Part C—Uninsured Motorists Coverage
- Part D—Coverage for Damage to Your Auto

PAP Liability Coverage

8. **Part A—Liability Coverage** will cover your legal liability (and that of other insureds under your policy) for bodily injury or property damage that arises out of ownership, use or maintenance of autos. For you, the named insured, and family members who live with you, this coverage is very broad and covers any auto specified by the policy provisions—such as a rental car, for example. Others, such as people who borrow your auto, are also covered, but on a more restrictive basis. In addition, the policy promises that the insurance company will defend you against lawsuits that arise from owning or using your auto or autos of others.

PAP Liability Coverage

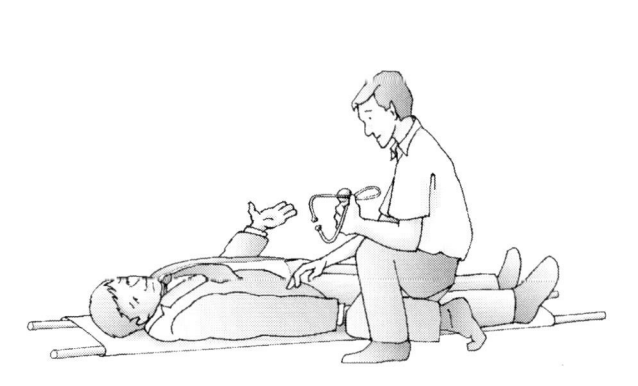

A PAP covers bodily injury...

...or property damage...

...caused by an auto accident...

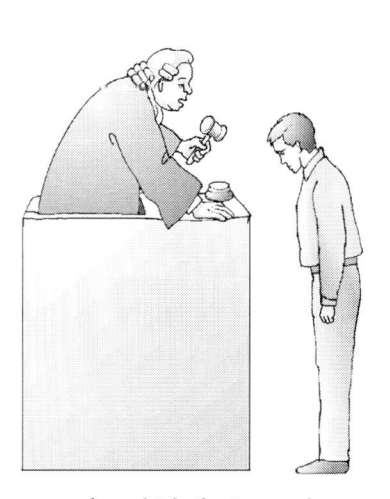

...for which the insured is legally responsible.

In which of the following situations would you be covered under the Liability coverage of your Personal Auto policy?

A. You lose control of your auto, and the corner of the front bumper creases the side of a parked car. Your auto isn't damaged, but there is damage to the parked car.

B. You're driving too fast and hit a pedestrian who is crossing the street at a crosswalk.

C. Another driver tries to squeeze an auto into a parking space that is too small and hits your parked auto.

D. You aren't paying attention, and your auto smashes into the rear of another auto when it stops suddenly. No one is injured, but the collision damages both autos.

Answer: A, B and D are correct. In D, only the damage to the other auto would be covered under Liability coverage.

PAP Medical Payments Coverage

9. **Part B—Medical Payments Coverage** will pay for medical bills and funeral expenses if you or your family members are struck by an auto or are injured in an auto accident. It will also pay for these expenses for a passenger who is injured or killed while occupying your auto. Unlike Liability coverage, Medical Payments coverage applies without regard to fault.

Who Is Insured for Medical Payments Coverage

Named Insured, Family Members, and Passengers in a Covered Auto

Named Insured and Family Members When Struck by an Auto

In which of the following situations would you be covered by Medical Payments coverage of your Personal Auto policy?

A. You brake suddenly to avoid hitting a child who has run into a street, and a passenger in your auto is injured.

B. Your auto slides on ice and hits a fence. A large section of the fence is destroyed.

C. You cause an auto accident in which two other vehicles are damaged.

D. You are injured when a truck jumps a curb and hits you as you're standing on a sidewalk.

Answer: A and D are correct.

PAP Uninsured Motorists Coverage

10. **Part C—Uninsured Motorists Coverage** (which is frequently referred to as UM coverage) is compulsory in some states—you must purchase it and may not reject it. Other states require insurance companies to offer UM coverage, but you can reject it if you wish. In still other states, UM coverage is not mandated by law but insurance companies offer it as an option.

    Uninsured Motorists coverage pays damages for bodily injury (and, in some states, pays for damage to your property) that result from an accident caused by the driver of an uninsured motor vehicle. Because the other driver has no auto Liability coverage from which you could collect, you may be reimbursed under your own UM coverage. An uninsured motor vehicle also includes a hit-and-run vehicle (the auto and its owner or driver are unknown).

    Suppose you're seriously injured in an auto accident when another driver runs a red light. The other driver has no auto liability insurance. Would your UM coverage help pay your medical bills?   ( ) Yes   ( ) No

Answer: Yes

PAP Coverage for Damage to Your Auto

11. **Part D—Coverage for Damage to Your Auto**, sometimes called **physical damage coverages**, will protect your auto and other autos in your custody from losses from a variety of perils. Two basic coverages are offered:

    - **Collision coverage**, which protects against damage that results from your auto's impact with another vehicle or object or the upset of your auto.

- **Other Than Collision (OTC) coverage**, which is traditionally known as **Comprehensive coverage** and covers just about every other type of auto physical damage loss except collision.

A. Which Personal Auto policy coverage would pay for damage to your auto that is a result of its impact with another vehicle or object?
  1. Liability coverage
  2. Collision coverage
  3. Uninsured Motorists coverage
  4. Comprehensive coverage

B. Which PAP coverage would pay for damage to your auto that is not the result of a collision?
  1. Liability coverage
  2. Collision coverage
  3. Uninsured Motorists coverage
  4. Comprehensive coverage

Answer: A. 2 is correct; B. 4 is correct.

Other Personal Lines Policies

12. There are a number of other personal lines policies that many people need to supplement their homeowners, dwelling or personal auto policies because they exclude certain perils or coverage for certain types of losses.

    - **Earthquake or flood insurance.** Homeowners and dwelling policies exclude coverage for earthquakes and floods because of the extra hazards they pose. You can purchase earthquake insurance and flood insurance separately or add them as endorsements to a homeowners or dwelling policy for payment of additional premium.

    - **Mobile home insurance.** Homeowners policies and some dwelling forms do not cover mobile homes. If you need mobile home insurance, you can purchase it through a separate policy or as an endorsement to a policy for payment of additional premium.

    - **Personal inland marine insurance.** You may own several expensive items of personal property, such as jewelry, furs, antiques, paintings, cameras, coin and stamp collections, and sports equipment. These items may not be adequately covered by your homeowners or dwelling policy because of certain limitations in the policy. Personal inland marine insurance can provide more comprehensive coverage for such personal property.

Inland marine insurance was developed from ocean marine insurance, which provides broad coverage for ships and goods being transported by water. Inland marine insurance got its name because it provides broad coverage for a wide range of property on land, no matter where on land it may be located. Personal inland marine policies include the Personal Articles Floater, Personal Property Floater and Personal Effects Floater. You can also add personal inland marine coverage to your homeowners or dwelling policy by endorsement and payment of additional premium.

- **Personal watercraft insurance.** Homeowners policies provide only limited coverage for boats of certain sizes with motors of certain horsepower. Dwelling policies only provide coverage for rowboats and canoes. If you own a boat, you may need more comprehensive coverage. Personal watercraft insurance, which you can obtain through a separate policy or by endorsement to your homeowners or dwelling policy, provides both liability and physical damage insurance for boats.

- **Personal umbrella liability insurance.** The Liability coverage in your personal insurance policies may not cover certain types of claims or may not provide coverage under certain circumstances. For example, homeowners policies only cover bodily injury and property damage liability. They don't cover injury that does not cause physical harm, such as mental anguish, humiliation, false arrest, libel, slander, or invasion of privacy. As another example, standard auto liability policies usually apply only to accidents and losses that occur in the U.S., Puerto Rico, Canada, and sometimes a limited area along the U.S. border of Mexico. If you cause an auto accident in southern Mexico, for example, your personal auto policy probably will not cover your liability.

    In addition, even though the purpose of liability insurance is to protect you from financial loss, there is a limit beyond which the company will not pay: the policy limits. If you are liable for damages, and your policy only pays part of those damages, up to its limits, you will have to pay the remainder. In today's society where lawsuits and high-dollar legal liability settlements are common occurrences, the remainder you would have to pay could wipe you out financially.

    Personal umbrella insurance forms an "umbrella" over a broad range of other liability insurance to provide you with high-limit supplemental liability protection for liability losses that would not otherwise be covered under your underlying policies and for catastrophic losses.

Ask your supervisor which personal lines coverages your company writes, if any, and list them here.

Match the description at the left with the type of insurance at the right.

___ A. Two types of insurance that provide coverage for perils that are excluded under homeowners and dwelling policies because of the extra hazards they pose.

___ B. Provides more comprehensive coverage on expensive items of personal property than is provided by homeowners and dwelling policies.

___ C. Provides more comprehensive coverage for boats than is available with homeowners and dwelling policies.

___ D. Provides high-limit supplemental liability protection for liability losses that are not covered or are not adequately covered by underlying personal liability insurance.

___ E. Excluded under homeowners and some dwelling policy forms, this coverage can be obtained as a separate policy or as an endorsement.

1. Flood insurance
2. Earthquake insurance
3. Mobile home insurance
4. Personal watercraft insurance
5. Personal inland marine insurance
6. Personal umbrella liability insurance

Answer: 1, 2 A.; 5 B.; 4 C.; 6 D.; 3 E.

COMMERCIAL LINES POLICIES

13. Businesses have many exposures to loss, just as do individuals. Many of these exposures are similar to those you have studied in relation to your personal insurance, but business exposures are more complex. If you're a businessowner, you run these risks:

A Businessowner's Potential Losses

Buildings Will Be Damaged Or Destroyed

Business Property, Such As Furniture, Fixtures, Equipment, And Inventory Will Be Damaged Or Destroyed

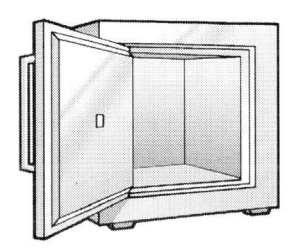

Business Property Will Be Stolen

Income Will Be Lost If The Business Has To Temporarily Shut Down Because Of A Loss

There Will Be Extra Expenses Involved In Keeping The Business Open And Operating After A Loss

There Will Be Legal Liability For Damages That Arise Out Of The Business Premises, Operations, Products, Contractual Obligations, Or Vehicles

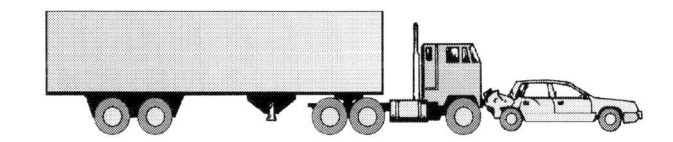

Vehicles Owned And Used In The Business Will Be Damaged Or Destroyed

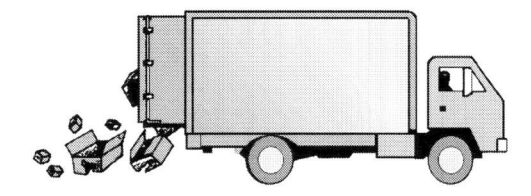

Business Property Will Be Damaged Or Destroyed While It's Being Transported

There are a great variety of insurance coverages that will protect you against losses of these types.

The Commercial Package Policy

14. As a businessowner, you can purchase a package of coverages, which together are called the **Commercial Package Policy (CPP)**, that cover many business exposures, instead of purchasing a number of individual policies. In this way, the insurance company may be able to offer you a package discount and reduce your premium. Of course, you can purchase these commercial coverages as separate policies if you don't wish to purchase a package policy.

Ask your supervisor if your company writes commercial package policies. If so, ask which coverages are available and list them here.

Not all commercial coverages are available as part of a CPP, however. The following illustration shows the primary available coverages. We'll discuss each of these as well as a few key coverages that may *only* be purchased separately.

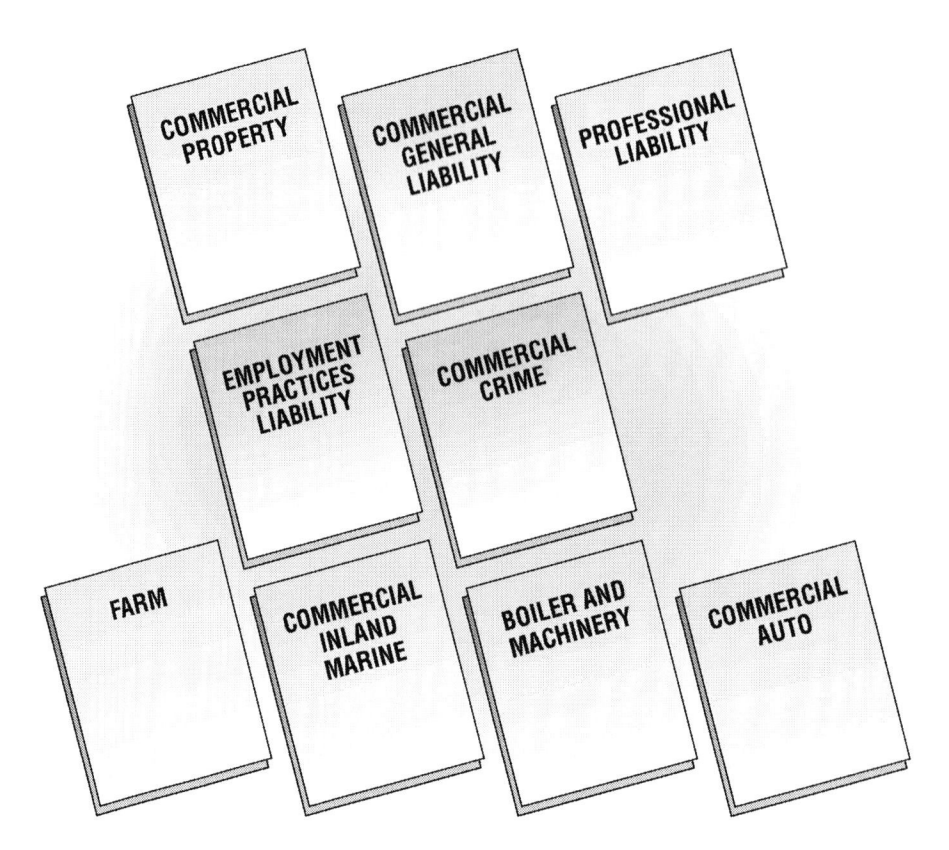

CPP Coverages Available

- COMMERCIAL PROPERTY
- COMMERCIAL GENERAL LIABILITY
- PROFESSIONAL LIABILITY
- EMPLOYMENT PRACTICES LIABILITY
- COMMERCIAL CRIME
- FARM
- COMMERCIAL INLAND MARINE
- BOILER AND MACHINERY
- COMMERCIAL AUTO

After you answer the following questions, we'll take a brief look at each of the CPP coverages.

A. If you purchase the Commercial Package policy, it can include
   1. any commercial insurance coverage you may desire as part of the package.
   2. only coverages that are available as part of a package, not separately.
   3. many commercial insurance coverages that can be packaged together.

B. Could you, as a businessowner, purchase only property and general liability coverages for your business through a CPP? ( ) Yes ( ) No

C. If you also wish commercial auto, commercial inland marine and commercial crime coverages, can you obtain them through a CPP?
( ) Yes ( ) No

Answer: A. 3 is correct; B. Yes; C. Yes

Commercial Property Coverage

15. You can purchase **Commercial Property coverage** as part of a CPP or as a separate policy. It covers commercial buildings and personal property against a wide variety of perils or causes of loss. There are several commercial property coverage forms:

Commercial Property Coverage Forms

Building And Personal Property Form

Covers Buildings, Business Personal Property And Property Of Others On The Insured's Premises

Condominium Forms

Covers Condominium Associations' Buildings And Permanent Fixtures And Commercial Condominium Unit Owners' Personal Property

Builders Risk Form

Provides Specialized Coverage For Buildings Under Construction

Business Income And Extra Expense Forms

Time Element Forms That Cover Loss Of Income When Operations Are Suspended Until Insured Damages Can Be Repaired Following A Loss And Provide Cash For Extra Charges Required To Keep A Business Operating After A Covered Loss

Match the description at the left with the commercial property form at the right.

___ A. Covers buildings, business personal property and property of others at a business premises

___ B. Cover condominium buildings and unit-owners' personal property

___ C. Covers commercial buildings under construction

___ D. Provide time element coverages after a covered loss

1. Builders Risk Form
2. Business Income And Extra Expense Forms
3. Building And Personal Property Form
4. Condominium Forms

Answer: 3 A.; 4 B.; 1 C.; 2 D.

Commercial General Liability Coverage

16. If you're a businessowner, you have business liability exposures just as you have personal liability exposures. Commercial liability exposures can include liability that arises out of:

    - Business premises
    - Business operations
    - Products
    - Completed operations
    - Contractual agreements

Commercial General Liability Coverage

Protects Businesses Against Legal Liability

You can cover most of these liability exposures under the **Commercial General Liability (CGL) form** as part of a CPP or under a separate policy. CGL insurance provides three basic coverages:

- **Liability coverage**, which protects you, as a businessowner, against liability for bodily injury and property damage that arises out of your business premises or business activities

- **Personal and Advertising Injury Liability coverage**, which covers your liability as a businessowner that arises out of specialized situations, such as libel (written defamation), slander (oral defamation), false arrest, wrongful entry, violation of privacy, use of another's advertising ideas, or infringement on copyrights, trade dress or slogans

- **Medical Payments coverage**, which covers medical bills for accidents that arise from your business activities, without regard to fault

The CGL form excludes liability that arises from performing professional services, such as those of a doctor or lawyer. Professional liability must be insured under specialized policies that are commonly referred to as **malpractice insurance** (for the medical profession) or **errors and omissions insurance** (for such professionals as lawyers, insurance agents and accountants).

Which of the following could be covered by CGL coverage?

A. Benning Corporation receives notice that it is being sued by a customer who was hurt by one of its products.

B. Hank Kandy, a dentist, is being sued by Janice Leery, a patient, who says Hank botched his work on her root canal.

C. The Burgeon Company is presented with a doctor bill from Fred Nearsight, a visitor, who was cut on broken glass when he mistook a full-length window for a door.

Answer: A and C are correct.

Farm Coverage

Farm Coverage Form

17. If you own a farm, your situation would be unique in that it would combine elements of both personal and commercial exposures to risk. The **Farm Coverage form** part of a CPP can provide the special coverage you would need.

Provides Both Farm Property Coverage And Farm Liability Coverage

Farm Property coverage covers your farm's:

- dwelling,
- personal property,
- business equipment, and
- farm structures.

Farm Liability coverage covers liability that arises out of:

- farm premises,
- personal activities, and
- business activities.

One type of coverage not provided under farm insurance is coverage for growing crops. This specialized coverage must be purchased under a **Crop-Hail policy**.

Assume you have a farm that is insured by a Farm Coverage form that covers tornado losses. A tornado strikes your farm and destroys the following property. Which parts of this loss would be covered under your Farm Coverage form, up to its limits?

A. Your home
B. Personal property in your home
C. Your barn
D. Farm equipment in your barn
E. Your unharvested wheat crop

Answer: A, B, C, and D are correct.

Commercial Crime Coverage

18. If you're a businessowner, you may have a broad exposure to crime, ranging from burglary and robbery to forgery, computer fraud and extortion. The **Commercial Crime Coverage form** of a CPP can provide a variety of crime coverages for both business property and money and securities. These are important coverages because most commercial property insurance limits or excludes these coverages.

Commercial Crime Coverages

You can purchase crime coverage for various types of property on and off your business premises. You can select from a number of coverages to cover a single crime peril or a group of perils. Among the specific coverages available are:

- Employee Theft
- Forgery or Alteration
- Inside the Premises—Theft of Money and Securities
- Inside the Premises—Robbery or Safe Burglary of Other Property
- Outside the Premises
- Computer Fraud
- Money Orders and Counterfeit Paper Currency

Commercial crime coverage may be used to insure against loss or damage to:

A. money.
B. securities.
C. business property while on or off the premises.
D. All of the above

Answer: D is correct.

Boiler and Machinery Coverage

19. Steam boilers and other types of power-generating or pressurized equipment, such as turbines, electric power transformers, and refrigeration systems, are specialized risks because of the extensive damage these machines can cause. If you have a business that uses any of these machines, you need **Boiler and Machinery insurance**. You can purchase it as part of a CPP or as a separate policy.

One of the important features of this coverage is its emphasis on loss prevention. As a requirement of coverage, insurance company engineers regularly inspect the boiler or other covered machine.

Why do you think an insurance company would want to provide inspection services as part Boiler and Machinery coverage?

A. It helps justify charging a higher premium.

B. The company automatically provides it as part of all commercial lines coverages.

C. It's a benefit to both the company and the insured because it can help prevent extensive losses that accidents that involve such machines can cause.

Answer: C is correct.

Commercial Auto Coverage

20. If you're a businessowner, you may have auto exposures that also need to be covered. **Commercial Auto Coverage forms** provide liability and physical damage coverages for vehicles a business owns, borrows, rents, leases, or hires.

    There are four major Commercial Auto Coverage forms:

Commercial Auto Forms

Business Auto Coverage Form

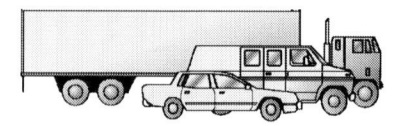

Covers Virtually All Commercial Auto Exposures Other Than Truckers (Who Haul Goods For Others) And Garage-Type Businesses, Such As Car Dealers Or Parking Garages

Garage Coverage Form

For Businesses Having Autos Of Others In Their Care, Custody Or Control, Such As Businesses That Sell, Service, Repair, Park Or Store Vehicles

Truckers Coverage Form

Covers Truckers That Haul Goods For Others, Subject To Special Trucking Industry Regulations

Motor Carrier Coverage Form

An Alternative To The Truckers Coverage Form, Covers Businesses That Transport Property By Auto, Not Just Businesses That Are Hired For That Purpose

Under which commercial auto coverage form(s) would the auto exposures of the following businesses be covered?

A. A small print shop _____

B. A trucking firm _____

C. An auto dealership _____

Answer: A. Business Auto; B. Truckers or Motor Carrier; C. Garage;

Commercial Inland Marine Coverage

21. As a businessowner, you might also need the broad coverage of **Commercial Inland Marine insurance**. There are a variety of forms, some of which can be written as part of a CPP while others must be written as separate policies.

Commercial Inland Marine Coverages

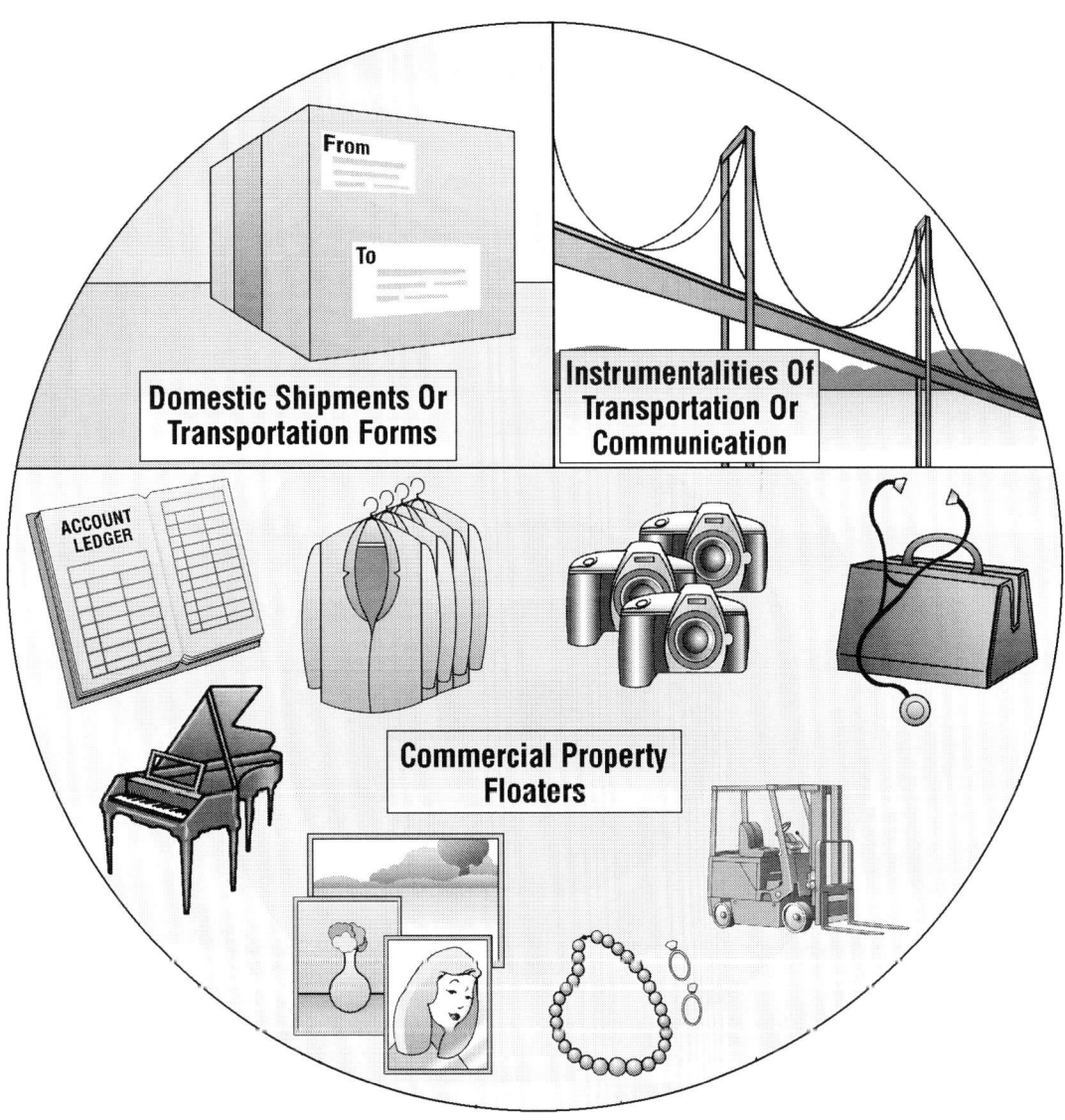

Commercial inland marine forms are divided into three main categories:

- **Domestic shipments.** The forms in this category are known as **Transportation forms.** They cover the shipper who has the goods sent or the carrier who transports the shipper's goods.

- **Instrumentalities of transportation or communication.** These forms cover such things as docks, piers, bridges, wharves, pipelines, and television towers.

- **Commercial property floaters.** The term "floater" has historically referred to policies that "follow" the property from location to location. There are a wide variety of policies in this category.

Among the commercial property floaters are the following:

- **Equipment floaters**, which cover various types of equipment, such as that of contractors, professional bands, rental companies, morticians, physicians, surgeons, dentists, salespeople, photographers, pattern and die manufacturers, and theater companies

- **Business floaters**, which cover property on exhibit, property in the care of commercial processors or contractors, property being installed or under construction, accounts receivable, valuable papers, electronic data processing equipment, and signs

- **Dealers policies**, which provide broad coverage for the merchandise of dealers such as dealers in jewelry, furs, cameras, musical instruments, fine art, stamps, and coins

- **Bailees policies**, which cover businesses, such as dry cleaners and shoe repairers, who regularly have customers' property in their possession for a specific purpose, such as repair or safekeeping

Match the property at the left with the type of commercial inland marine insurance that would cover it at the right.

____ A. Goods being shipped by truck
____ B. A dentist's equipment
____ C. A business's accounts receivable records
____ D. A fur dealer's merchandise
____ E. Customers' property left for cleaning at a dry cleaner

1. Bailees policy
2. Transportation form
3. Business floater
4. Equipment floater
5. Dealers policy

Answer: 2 A.; 4 B.; 3 C.; 5 D.; 1 E.

Professional Liability Insurance

22. As a businessowner, you may have professional liability exposures that need to be covered. **Professional Liability insurance** covers liability arising out

of rendering or failing to render services of a professional nature. Professionals have two kinds of legal duty to their clients. These are to perform the services for which they were hired and to perform them in accordance with the appropriate standards of conduct. Because of their special skills, professionals are held to a higher standard of conduct.

Professional Liability policies can go by several different names. **Malpractice insurance** is the term commonly applied to Medical Professional Liability policies written for medical professionals or institutions, including physicians, nurses, dentists, surgeons, opticians, optometrists, chiropractors, and veterinarians. **Errors and Omissions (E&O) insurance** is a broad term that refers to Professional Liability policies written for other professionals, such as insurance agents, accountants, architects, stockbrokers, engineers, consultants, and attorneys.

Another type of Professional Liability policy, the **Fiduciary Liability policy**, protects those who manage private pension and employee benefit plans against liability for violation of the ERISA law.

A. Professional Liability insurance written for medical professionals and institutions is commonly described as _____ insurance.

B. Professional Liability insurance written for insurance agents is frequently called _____ insurance.

Answer: A. Malpractice; B. Errors And Omissions (E&O)

Employment Practices Liability Insurance

23. If you're a businessowner, you may have exposures to wrongful termination, discrimination, sexual harassment, and other employment-related practices. This coverage is provided by **Employment Practices Liability (EPL) insurance**.

    Although standard ISO forms are available for this type of insurance, many companies issue their own policies. One result of this is that policy provisions vary greatly among insurers. Most policies cover wrongful acts committed by the employer and its employees. Typical exclusions include:

    - Wrongful termination practices committed with dishonest, fraudulent, criminal or malicious intent

    - Mass layoffs of employees

    - Deliberate fraud or purposeful violations of laws, rules or regulations

    - Bodily injury or property damage other than emotional distress, mental anguish or humiliation

    - Liabilities of others assumed under contract, except employment contracts

    - Circumstances reported under prior EPL policies

Which of the following is not true about Employment Practices Liability coverage?

A. It is always written on the standard ISO form.
B. It usually excludes deliberate violations of law.
C. It covers acts committed by an employer, but not its employees.

Answer: A and C are correct.

Workers' Compensation and Employers Liability Coverage

24. Employers are required by state **workers' compensation laws** to pay the medical bills, lost wages and other expenses incurred by employees who are injured while on the job. The **Workers' Compensation and Employers Liability policy** provides businesses with the coverage state law requires for injured workers.

Workers' Compensation and Employers Liability Coverages

The policy also includes Liability coverage for the employer if he or she must pay damages under common law when an employee sues for amounts in addition to those required under the workers' compensation law.

Medical bills of which of the following would be covered under the employer's Workers' Compensation and Employers Liability policy?

A. A factory worker fractures an arm while working on an assembly line.
B. A secretary is injured in an accident while driving to work one morning.

Answer: A is correct (the policy only covers work-related injuries).

Other Commercial Lines Policies

25. Other important commercial lines policies are:

    - **Businessowners-type (BOP) policies.** These are package policies that cover small service, retail or manufacturing businesses that meet specific eligibility requirements. BOPs contain some, but not all, of the coverages provided by the CPP. Unlike the CPP, BOPs are prepackaged policies that contain certain key property and liability coverages, and the insured cannot select the coverages that can be included.

    - **Commercial Umbrella Liability policies.** These policies, like the personal umbrella liability policies you studied earlier, form an "umbrella" over a broad range of other liability insurance to provide you with high-limit supplemental liability protection for liability losses that would not otherwise be covered under your underlying policies and for catastrophic losses.

    - **Ocean Marine policies.** This is one of the earliest forms of insurance and was developed to cover exposures related to transporting goods over water. These policies can cover damage to a ship's cargo, damage to the ship and liability for damage or injury caused by the ship.

Match the exposure at the left with the type of coverage at the right.

___ A. Tivoli Corporation needs coverage for a potentially huge liability loss not covered by its CGL policy.

___ B. Hawkin, Inc., has the typical insurance needs of a small retail business.

___ C. The Bergen Company's business is shipping goods between seaports.

1. Businessowners-type policy
2. Commercial Umbrella Liability policy
3. Ocean marine policy

Answer: 2 A.; 1 B.; 3 C.

Ask your supervisor if your company writes commercial lines and, if so, which policies are available. List those policies here.

Now you have some important basic information about the property-casualty insurance industry and its products. In the next unit, we'll build on some of this information as we talk about improving the public's and our own understanding of insurance.

UNIT 7

Improving Understanding of Insurance

1. In this unit, we'll talk about what you can do to improve both our own and the public's understanding of the insurance product and the insurance industry. While it isn't necessary for everyone to know all the ins and outs of every policy, it is important to have a clear message of what insurance is all about in your mind and to be able to communicate that message to others through the work you do. In discussing that message, we'll cover:

    - the reasons why most people do not readily understand insurance;

    - the efforts that the industry has made and will continue to make to improve understanding of insurance on the part of insurance professionals and the public; and

    - the answers to some questions that people often ask about insurance.

    When you're finished with this unit, your study of this text will be done. But you'll have only begun on your career in the exciting world of insurance!

WHY INSURANCE ISN'T READILY UNDERSTOOD

2. People don't readily understand insurance for a number of reasons.

People Often Have Questions About Insurance

- **Insurance is an intangible product.** Insurance isn't a tangible product like a watermelon or a gemstone or a car—you can't thump it for ripeness, hold it up to the light, or take it for a test drive before you buy it. Insurance is a concept, a promise. The promise is printed on paper, but that's only the evidence of the agreement between the insured and the insurance company. The product itself is protection against financial loss. And that's not an object that you can see or hold in your hands.

    At first glance, intangible products seem like they would be harder to grasp than tangible ones. But it's relatively easy to make insurance more "real"—and more interesting—to people by using examples and illustrations to explain ideas. Remember our fictional town of Middlefield in Unit 2? It made the definition of insurance easier and more fun for you to learn (and for us to write about).

- **Insurance is a complex business.** There are many different insurance companies, policies and people involved in this business. It's easy for all this diversity to overwhelm people.

  But they don't have to be overwhelmed. There are some general concepts of insurance—such as risk-sharing and pure versus speculative risk—on which everything is based. By relating to a few basic concepts, you and others can better understand the insurance industry's diversity.

- **Insurance deals with a subject that people tend to avoid.** People don't like to think about the chance of experiencing a loss. They may have insurance, but they hope they'll never have to "use" it, so they usually don't even read their policies. Avoiding the subject naturally contributes to a lack of understanding about insurance.

  But insurance plays many roles in our lives even if no loss ever occurs. It gives us peace of mind to know that our financial stability is ensured. It protects lenders' interests so we can buy homes and cars and start or expand businesses. It contributes jobs, tax dollars and investments to our communities and national economy. Being aware of these positive aspects of insurance increases people's willingness to learn more about it.

Match the reason people don't readily understand insurance with the strategy for overcoming it.

____ A. Insurance is intangible.
____ B. Insurance is complex.
____ C. People avoid the subject.

1. Look for positive aspects
2. Find examples and illustrations
3. Relate to basic concepts

Answer: 2 A.; 3 B.; 1 C.

DOING SOMETHING ABOUT IT

3. The insurance industry has taken the initiative to make itself and its product better understood. These efforts fall into two categories: communication and service.

   - **Improving Communication:** The insurance industry is opening a number of lines of communication designed to improve understanding. Companies and trade groups have produced video programs that discuss issues of interest to consumers and that are shown on television and to gatherings of people. Companies have rewritten their policies to remove jargon and make use of everyday language so that they are easier to read. Companies are sponsoring training programs like this one to help their employees better understand their business. And they are encouraging their employees to share that understanding not only with insureds and others they meet on the job, but also with their friends, neighbors and relatives.

- **Improving Service**: Better understanding comes not just from hearing what people say, but also from seeing what they do. The industry's response to Hurricane Andrew, which we described in Unit 1, was not an isolated instance. The industry mounted similar efforts for other catastrophic losses in recent years, such as the California earthquakes, the Northeastern blizzard and the Midwest floods. In addition, the industry is constantly working to improve the quality and timeliness of the service it provides on routine claims.

You can also play a role in this worthwhile effort. By doing the best you can at your job, and by talking to the people you know about your job, you can help people understand insurance better.

In the next section, we'll look at some often-asked questions about insurance, and we'll provide the answers. In answering these questions, we'll be building on some of the knowledge you've already gained in this course.

Which of the following statements best describes the insurance industry's efforts to improve public understanding of insurance?

A. It is all talk, no action.

B. It has concentrated on giving good service without trying to explain what insurance is all about.

C. It has tried to send people a positive message about insurance through both words and deeds.

Answer: C is correct.

QUESTIONS PEOPLE OFTEN ASK ABOUT INSURANCE

Isn't Insurance Like Gambling?

4. People sometimes say that insurance is like gambling—that buying a policy is like betting against the insurance company that a loss will occur. That idea is mistaken. It doesn't take into account the difference between *pure* risk and *speculative* risk.

As you may recall from Unit 2, a *pure* risk involves the possibility of loss only, while a *speculative* risk involves the possibility of either loss or gain. Insurance covers only pure risks. If a loss occurs, an insured doesn't gain anything. Remember the principle of indemnity? The insured is simply restored to the same financial condition he or she enjoyed prior to the loss.

Insurance Is Not Like Gambling

Insurable risks are those where there is a chance of loss only—not gain.

Gambling is, of course, a speculative risk. You either lose the money you bet or you get back more than you bet. That's *not* the case with insurance. So insurance is not like gambling.

In addition, gambling increases risk while insurance reduces risk. In gambling, no risk exists for you until you create it by placing a bet. At that point you assume a risk. In insurance, the risk exists already. By buying an insurance policy, you transfer the risk to the insurance company. So insurance is actually the *opposite* of gambling.

Which of the following statements describes a situation involving speculative risk?

A. John pays a $400 premium for one year's worth of property insurance coverage on his home; he files no claims that year.

B. Donna pays a $400 premium for one year's worth of property coverage on her home; after a tornado hits her home, the insurance company reimburses her for the cost of repairs in the amount of $55,000.

C. Ed wagers $100 with a friend that his favorite team will win the National Basketball League championship; his team wins and Ed's friend pays him $100.

Answer: C is correct.

If I Never Have a Claim, Haven't I Wasted My Money?

5. Some people feel that they've wasted their money if they pay for insurance and never have a claim. But, let's go back to our imaginary town of Middlefield and see if that's true.

   As you may recall, all 200 homeowners in Middlefield pay $500 a year to insure their $100,000 homes with ABC Insurance Company. Every year, one of those homes burns down. Let's say that you live in Middlefield, and one year the home that burns down belongs to the family next door. Here is their story as you observe it firsthand.

   One night the sound of sirens passing your house awakens you. You look out the window to find your neighbors huddling on the curb outside as they watch their home go up in flames. You give them what help you can, but the next few days are very chaotic for them as they essentially start their lives over. They settle in a motel and gradually start replacing the clothes and other things that the fire destroyed and that they need to get through each day. When you see your neighbors over the next few weeks, they complain about how their work and the children's grades at school are suffering because of the disruption in their lives.

   Eventually they settle into a somewhat normal routine, and after a couple months, their home is rebuilt and they move back into it. ABC Insurance Company sends them a check that covers the cost of repairs to their house and all their extra living expenses. But it can't replace the photographs, videos, and other mementos that were lost in the fire, nor does it compensate them for the inconvenience they've endured for the past few months.

   You and your neighbors each paid $500 to ABC Insurance Company. Your neighbors got $100,000 back. But who were the lucky ones? Would you trade places with your neighbors?

Sweet Dreams

Insurance gives peace of mind, whether or not a loss occurs.

Note that ABC didn't simply "keep" the $500 you paid for insurance. The company combined your premium with the $500 everyone else in Middlefield paid in order to reimburse your neighbors for their losses. To say that ABC "made" $500 on your policy and "lost" $95,500 on your neighbors' policy doesn't really explain how insurance works. Properly understood, ABC acted as a vehicle for pooling the resources of 200 homeowners so that the losses of one could be shared.

But what did you get for your $500? You got the peace of mind of knowing that if the sirens had stopped in front of your house that night, you wouldn't have had to bear the financial loss alone. Insurance is about more than just dealing with losses as they occur. In a broader sense, insurance is about dealing with *risk*—the *chance that a loss may occur*. Not everybody suffers a loss, but everybody *runs the risk* of suffering a loss. That's why every insured benefits from insurance. Even those who don't suffer losses receive the benefit of replacing the unknown costs of large losses with the known (and smaller) expense of the premium.

Place a check next to the following individual if he or she received full value for his or her insurance premium.

A. Helga paid a $400 auto insurance premium and never had a claim.

B. Bert paid a $400 auto insurance premium; his car collided with another vehicle and caused $4,000 worth of damage, for which he was liable. His insurance company paid the bill.

Answer: A and B are correct.

Why Are My Rates Going Up?

6. The cost of a product is a major concern to any consumer. But, many insurance buyers don't understand the cost of insurance very well. For example, you may hear people say, "I've never had a claim—why are my rates going up?" Or, "I've paid more in premium than I've gotten back in claims—why does the company need more money from me?"

    You can understand why some people make such comments, but the fact is that an individual's policy isn't priced according to that individual's experience. It's the *group's* experience that determines the cost of coverage. While low-risk groups pay lower premiums than high-risk groups, even low-risk groups aren't immune from factors like inflation, increasing litigation of claims and mounting insurance fraud that cause claim costs to rise. If claim costs rise, premiums must increase to cover them.

To get a clearer picture of how costs drive rates, study the following illustration.

Insurance Company Cash Flow

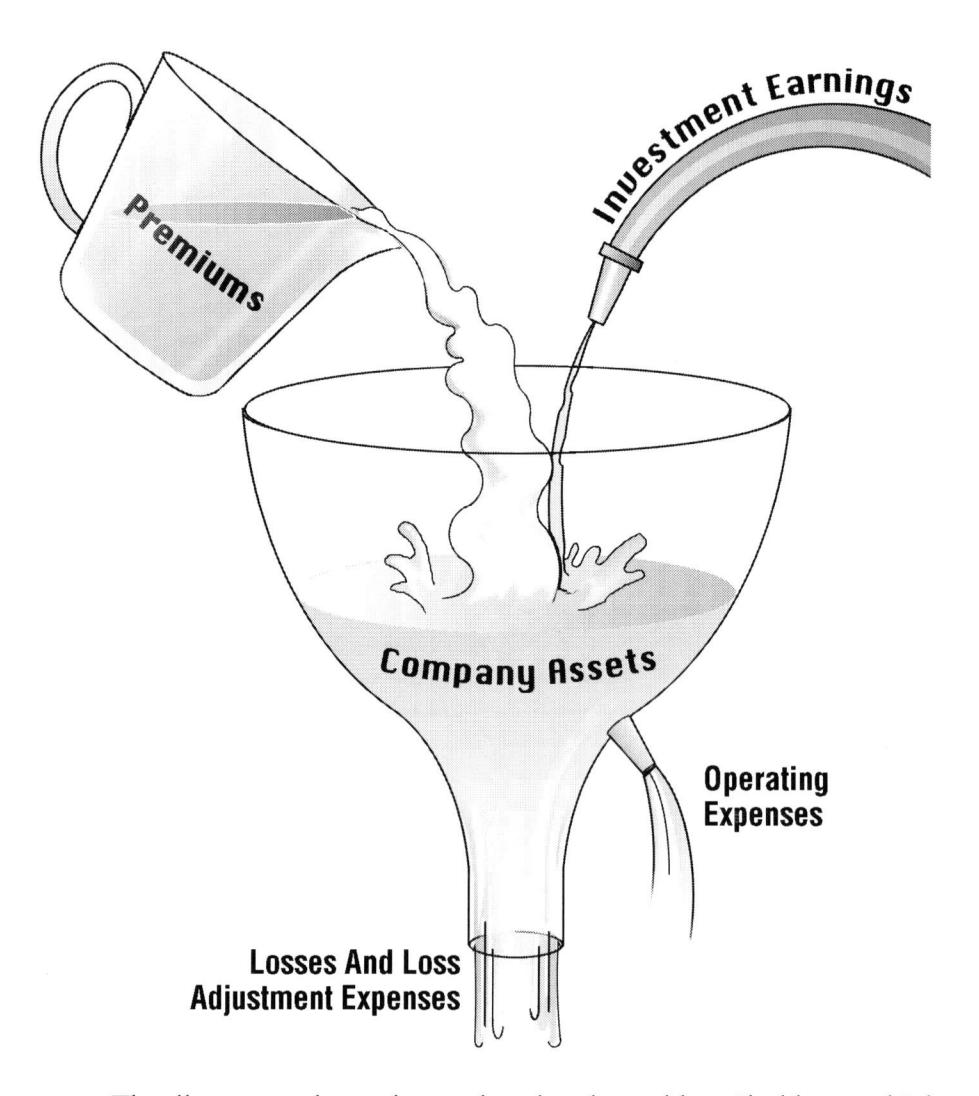

The illustration shows that, rather than being like a "holding tank" for assets, an insurance company is actually more like a funnel. With money continually flowing out the bottom in order to pay for insureds' losses and the company's operating expenses, it's important to maintain an adequate flow of funds into the company. While investment earnings make a significant contribution, premiums are the main source of insurance company income. If premiums are inadequate, it may not be long until an insurance company's assets drop to an unsatisfactory level.

The preceding illustration shows that the largest outflow of dollars from an insurance company is _____.

Answer: losses and loss adjustment expenses

7. Some people wonder why insurance companies must maintain a certain level of assets. They may ask, "Why not use some of those assets to pay increasing claim costs instead of raising my premium?" There are a number of reasons:

- **Loss experience isn't steady.** When catastrophes strike, or when claim costs go up unexpectedly for any other reason, losses will exceed premium income. Insurers need assets to draw on in such cases in order to make prompt payments to insureds who have suffered losses.

- **Assets are set aside against future liabilities.** When an insurer accepts a premium, it agrees to pay for covered losses that occur. Using the law of large numbers, the insurer can predict that a given number of losses are fairly certain to occur, although the insurer can't know precisely when and to whom they will occur. For that reason, it makes sense to begin setting aside some money now to pay for those losses.

- **Investment earnings on assets reduce the amount of premium needed to maintain adequate cash flow.** If an insurer had no assets, it would have no investment earnings from those assets. Without investment earnings to help pay for losses and expenses, premiums would be relatively higher. Maintaining a strong asset base helps keep premiums as low as they can be.

Some people wonder why insurers can't manage claim costs better in order to keep from having to raise rates. They may even say that insurers don't try to minimize the cost of losses since they just pass the cost on to insureds in the form of higher premiums. But, such assertions aren't based in fact. Insurers have to compete with each other for consumers' business, and they know that consumers base their buying decisions to a large extent on cost. To keep their premiums competitive, insurers work hard to manage claim costs. For example:

- Workers' compensation insurers attempt to reduce costs by managing medical care and by helping injured workers recover faster so they may return to productivity sooner.

- Many auto insurers promote the use of safety and anti-theft equipment by offering discounts on autos that have them.

- Many personal property insurers offer similar discounts for homes that have smoke alarms, dead bolts, fire extinguishers and other such devices.

- Many commercial property insurers make inspection and loss control a regular part of their business, as we've mentioned, and they also offer discounts for such safety equipment as sprinkler and alarm systems and for watch persons on the premises and certain types of safes.

- Insurers of all kinds are actively combating fraud by investigating suspicious claims and lobbying for stiffer penalties for offenders.

Some people also point to insurer operating expenses as the cause of rising rates. They say that insurers don't try to control their own costs of doing business. But, in order to have competitive rates, insurers know they have to operate efficiently as well as manage claim costs. Insurance is a business, and it is subject to the same rules of the marketplace as any other business. Consumers seek value—the best product for the money. So, as with any business that wants to remain competitive, insurers are always seeking to identify and implement ways to cut their operating expenses. They know they have to operate efficiently.

Ask your supervisor or trainer for examples of ways your company tries to manage its claim costs and operating expenses.

Which of the following statements are true?
A. In general, if claim costs increase, premiums must also increase.
B. The investment earnings on company assets help keep premiums lower.
C. Insurers don't try to manage claim costs since they just pass these costs on to insureds in the form of higher premiums.
D. Insurers continually try to find ways to operate more efficiently in order to keep their premiums competitive.

Answer: A, B and D are correct.

How Are My Premium Payments Used?

8. Some people think that with all the premiums being collected, insurance companies must have large earnings. But, a look at the figures shows that isn't the case.

    The following illustration depicts the average insurer's income, expenses and earnings. These figures are based on consolidated results for the entire property-casualty insurance industry. While operating results vary somewhat from year to year and from company to company, the figures shown are typical for recent years.

Income, Expenses and Earnings

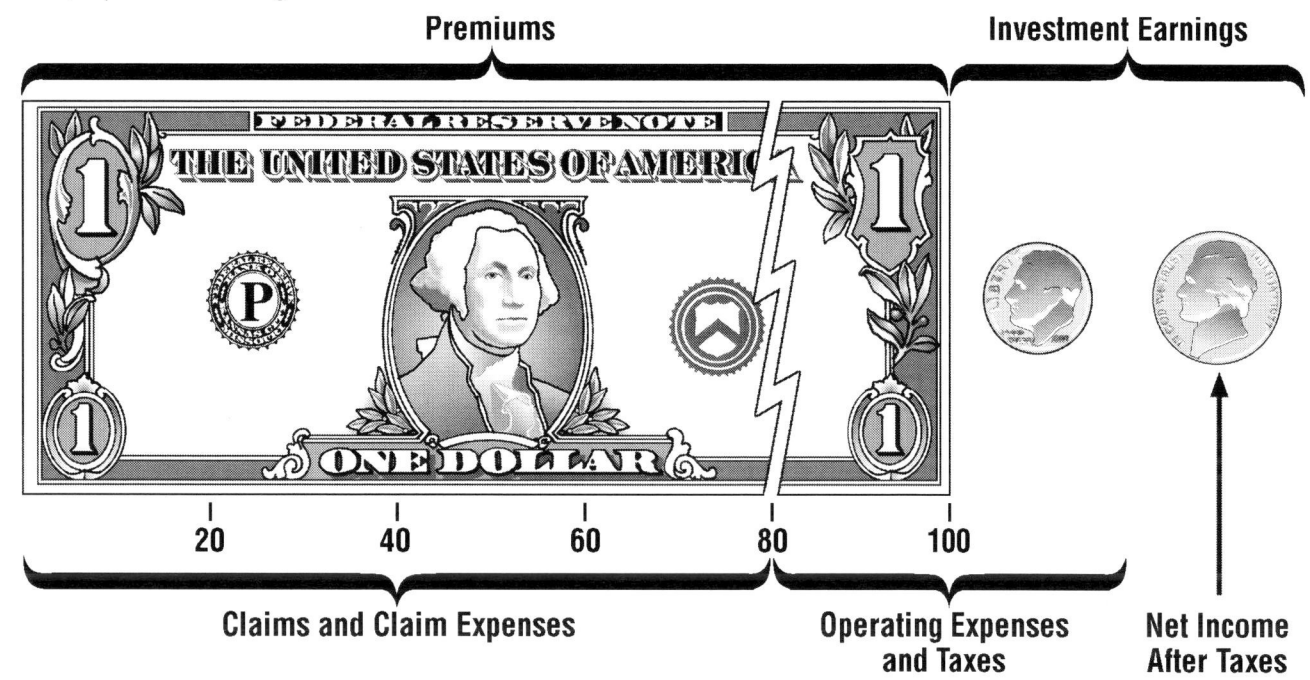

Premiums — 20, 40, 60, 80

Investment Earnings — 100

Claims and Claim Expenses

Operating Expenses and Taxes

Net Income After Taxes

The illustration shows that for every dollar in premium collected, investment earnings add about 15 cents to insurance company income. Out of that total amount, about 80 cents is paid out in claims and claim expenses. Another 30 cents goes to pay the company's operating expenses and taxes. That leaves about 5 cents of net income after taxes.

Insurance companies use these figures to calculate ratios that help them keep an eye on their financial results. One of the most important ratios companies use is the **loss ratio**, which is found by dividing losses (and loss expenses) by earned premiums. In our illustration, the loss ratio is 80 divided by 100, or 80%.

Another important ratio is the **expense ratio**, which is found by dividing operating expenses by premiums written. In our illustration, the expense ratio is 30 divided by 100, or 30%. (Note that the loss ratio uses *earned* premium and the expense ratio uses *written* premium. As you may remember from Unit 2, a company will have slightly more written premium than earned premium, but to keep things simple, we've ignored this small difference in our illustration.)

The loss ratio and the expense ratio are put together to form the **combined ratio**. In our illustration, the combined ratio is 80% plus 30%, or 110%. A combined ratio of 100% means that premium income roughly matches losses and expenses. When the combined ratio is over 100%, it indicates that premium income alone is not sufficient to pay losses and expenses, and that investment earnings are being relied on to cover outflows. In such a situation, if there are any earnings, they are coming from investments, not from premiums.

Some people say that companies are making more money than they appear to be because they use the complexities of insurance accounting to hide earnings. But, insurance accounting practices are defined by law and monitored by state and federal regulatory agencies. Admittedly, insurance accounting is complex, especially to the average consumer. But to knowledgeable regulators (and in the case of stock companies, savvy investors), insurance company financial results are an open book.

Assume ABC Insurance Company has the following financial results:

Written Premium:	$1,040,000
Earned Premium:	1,000,000
Investment Earnings:	125,000
Losses and Loss Expenses:	750,000
Operating Expenses:	260,000

A. The loss ratio for ABC is _____%.
B. The expense ratio for ABC is _____%.
C. The combined ratio for ABC is _____%.

Answer: A. 75% (losses of $750,000 divided by earned premium of $1,000,000); B. 25% (operating expenses of $260,000 divided by written premium of $1,040,000); C. 100% (loss ratio of 75% plus expense ratio of 25%)

Congratulations! You have now finished your study of this text. The things you've learned about the insurance industry will form a firm foundation of knowledge for you to build on in your insurance career. Now, when you talk to your friends, neighbors and relatives, you can let them know about the great industry in which you work. You can help them understand how insurance works and the contributions it makes to our economy, their communities, and their lives. Working in the insurance business gives you many opportunities to make a positive impact on your world.

You are now ready to test the knowledge you've gained by taking the course examination. We wish you luck and success in all your efforts.

Review Test

Important Information Regarding This Review Test

This exam was designed to provide accurate and authoritative information in regard to the subject matter covered. It is sold with the understanding that the publisher is not engaged in rendering legal, accounting, or other professional service. If legal advice or other expert assistance is required, the services of a competent professional person should be sought.

This text is updated periodically to reflect changes in laws and regulations. To verify that you have the most recent update, you may call Kaplan Financial Education at 1-800-423-4723.

1. People benefit from insurance in many ways. Which one of the following examples describes the way insurance helps policyholders maintain their financial stability?
   A. The restaurant where Janet Lee works caught fire, but she was able to return to work quickly because UVW Insurance Company's timely payment of the claim helped repairs progress without delay.
   B. Harvey Allen receives a $2,500 check from DEF Insurance Company to reimburse him for damage his car sustained in an accident.
   C. ABC Insurance Company employs 500 people in the city where its home office is located.
   D. XYZ Insurance Company pays $1 million in premium taxes to its state of domicile.

2. Suppose a business was uninsured and failed to reopen after it was destroyed by a fire. Which one of these statements is NOT correct?
   A. The local government that received tax revenue from the business would be affected by this loss.
   B. Only the owner of the restaurant would be affected by this loss.
   C. The owners who had their money invested in the business would be affected by this loss.
   D. The suppliers who sold goods and services to the business would be affected by this loss.

3. Which one of the following statements is NOT true about the benefits of insurance ownership?
   A. The benefits of insurance flow only to those who own it.
   B. The public benefits from the large amounts of tax revenue that are generated by insurance activities.
   C. The economy benefits from the large amounts of capital invested by insurance companies.
   D. Communities benefit from insurance ownership by businesses because a flow of economic activity can resume more quickly after a loss.

4. Which of the following expresses the best approach for the insurance industry to take toward losses experienced by insureds?
   A. The only service insurers should provide to insureds is the mailing of a check for a covered loss.
   B. Though insurers should respond promptly to claims resulting from isolated causes, they should move slowly in responding to catastrophes because of the large losses that may be involved.
   C. Every loss, whether it results from a natural disaster or a cause that isn't particularly newsworthy, is someone's catastrophe and deserves a quick and caring response from insurers.
   D. Since natural disasters get the most media coverage, only claims resulting from such catastrophes deserve the industry's best efforts.

5. Which one of the following statements is true regarding the loss prevention activities of insurers?
   A. Insurers are heavily involved in loss prevention activities, a tradition that has continued in the United States since colonial times.
   B. Insurers used to be involved in loss prevention activities but have ceased that involvement since about 1920.
   C. Insurers have never been involved in loss prevention activities.
   D. Insurers have only recently become involved in loss prevention activities.

6. In order to get a loan to buy a car, John had to obtain insurance on the car. The purpose of the insurance requirement is to
   A. protect the lender's financial interest in the car in the event it is damaged or destroyed.
   B. create an additional source of revenue for the lender.
   C. include the insurance company as a cosigner on the loan in case John defaults on his payments.
   D. prove to the lender that John has a sense of responsibility toward his obligations.

7. The insurance industry employs millions of people and pays billions in tax revenue to the federal and state government. These are two examples of how the insurance industry
   A. helps prevent losses.
   B. contributes to the nation's economic well-being.
   C. provides financial security for insureds.
   D. restores economic stability after catastrophic losses.

8. Probably the best reason for people to purchase insurance is to
   A. make money from every loss.
   B. get reimbursement for any loss, regardless of size.
   C. protect themselves from a significant financial loss.
   D. gamble with an insurance company regarding whether they will experience a loss.

9. You ask an insurance agent, "How much is the premium for this policy?" You are interested in knowing how much you would
   A. pay the insurer for the insurance policy.
   B. have to pay in additional charges to obtain an excluded coverage.
   C. receive should you decide to cancel the policy if you no longer require the coverage.
   D. collect for any loss you might sustain.

10. In most areas of the country, fire insurance continues to be one of a consumer's best buys. Which one of the following statements best explains the reason for this?
    A. The cost is feasible compared to the amount of insurance being purchased.
    B. Fire losses are generally not accidental.
    C. The cost of a loss is difficult to calculate.
    D. Fire losses occur to large numbers of people simultaneously.

11. Which group of words could best be used to construct a definition of insurance?
    A. Device to ensure that property remains in good condition—returns more to the insured than was paid in
    B. Savings account—many pay in—at least the amount paid in is returned to the individual
    C. Transfers risk of loss—many share the losses of a few
    D. Money paid to a company—paid back to an individual for any loss—certainty for certainty

12. The law of large numbers refers to which principle stated below?
    A. Losses are reduced if spread over large areas of the population.
    B. Large amounts of money collected by the insurance company will compensate any insured for any possible loss.
    C. To be insurable, a loss must occur to a large number of people at the same time.
    D. The larger the sample, the more accurate the prediction.

13. Which of the following is a definition of risk?
    A. The possibility of loss
    B. The cause of loss
    C. Anything that increases the chances of a loss
    D. A device that allows the losses that occur to a relatively small number of people to be shared among the members of a large group

14. George wants insurance to indemnify himself for the gradual wearing out of the roof on his house. Which answer choice below best completes the reason that such a loss would be difficult to insure? This loss would not be
    A. a risk to a sufficient number of people.
    B. calculable.
    C. catastrophic.
    D. accidental in nature.

15. Which one of the following is NOT a requirement for a risk to be insurable?
    A. A large number of people with similar potential for loss
    B. A loss that is accidental in nature
    C. A large number of people experiencing the loss at the same time
    D. A definite loss, difficult to counterfeit

16. The average person's methods of managing risk include all of the following EXCEPT
    A. rejecting the risk.
    B. transferring the risk.
    C. controlling the risk.
    D. avoiding the risk.

17. The difference between a pure risk and a speculative risk is that
    A. a speculative risk is insurable, while a pure risk is not.
    B. a pure risk involves the possibility of loss only, while a speculative risk involves the possibility of either loss or gain.
    C. a speculative risk is more likely to occur than a pure risk.
    D. a pure risk is created by the person involved, while a speculative risk is inherent in the ownership of some property.

18. Danny decides that he would like to get a piece of the action by buying part of an insurance policy covering the United Nations building in New York. He figures that if the building burns, he would collect some money. Of course, this is an impossible plan because
    A. the principle of subrogation prevents the payment of money to those not directly involved with the loss.
    B. Danny has no insurable interest in the United Nations building.
    C. insurance is primarily based on the theory of substituting certainty for uncertainty.
    D. the United Nations building is one of the world's truly fireproof buildings.

19. The principle of indemnity is expressed in which of the following sentences?
    A. A loss must be large enough to create a financial burden for the insured in order for it to be insurable.
    B. The insured should be restored financially to approximately the same position he or she was in prior to the loss.
    C. The insured should always receive less than the cost of a loss so he or she does not profit from the loss.
    D. An insured should always receive payment equal to the limits set forth in the policy.

20. Jared and Miranda Ashram purchased a $150,000 house. They paid $30,000 as a down payment and borrowed the remaining $120,000. In regard to the insurance on the Ashrams' home, this is an example of
    A. joint insurable interest.
    B. compounded equity.
    C. subrogation.
    D. indemnification.

21. The type of insurance designed to handle the risk of financial loss due to premature death or outliving one's financial resources is
    A. casualty insurance.
    B. health and disability insurance.
    C. life insurance.
    D. property insurance.

22. All of the following are types of property loss EXCEPT
    A. loss of income due to the loss of the property.
    B. liability for damage to another's property.
    C. additional expenses caused by the loss of the property.
    D. loss to the property itself.

23. The casualty line of insurance includes
    A. protection against the risk of financial loss due to premature death or outliving one's financial resources.
    B. a wide variety of coverages, one of the most important of which is liability insurance.
    C. liability insurance only.
    D. protection against loss to property only.

24. In order to be held legally liable for damages, an individual must generally be guilty of
    A. negligence.
    B. indemnification.
    C. a crime.
    D. insurance fraud.

25. Which one of the following represents a liability loss for the insured?
    A. The insured knows his pet ferret is likely to bite, yet he lets the ferret run loose and it bites a neighbor.
    B. The insured's home is damaged when the furnace explodes.
    C. Lightning kills a large oak tree in the insured's yard.
    D. The insured is injured in a car accident when another driver runs a red light.

26. Failing to use proper care in personal actions is also known as
    A. casualty.
    B. negligence.
    C. misdemeanor.
    D. liability.

27. The All Territory Fire & Casualty Company says that its stock is now selling for $34 a share. If you purchased insurance from this company, you would
    A. be part of a large voluntary association that writes a variety of insurance.
    B. become a stockholder in the company.
    C. not be required to purchase stock in the company.
    D. agree to share in the operating losses of the company.

28. You see an advertisement in a newspaper urging you to buy insurance from an agent representing Stearman Mutual Insurance Company. If you purchase your insurance from this company, you would
    A. agree to insure everyone else in the company.
    B. be able to purchase stock from the company.
    C. not be able to vote for the management of the company.
    D. automatically own and control a portion of the company.

29. All members of a club to which you belong agree to insure each other, sharing all of the losses or profits. This would be known as a
    A. reciprocal company.
    B. mutual company.
    C. Lloyd's association.
    D. stock company.

30. A group of private individuals voluntarily agrees to write insurance for a variety of risks. This type of company is known as a
    A. reciprocal company.
    B. stock company.
    C. Lloyd's association.
    D. mutual company.

31. The Stormy Mutual Insurance Company of Omaha, Nebraska, is licensed to sell insurance in Illinois, Indiana, and Iowa. In these three states, it is a/an _____ insurer.
    A. domestic
    B. admitted
    C. alien
    D. nonadmitted

32. The Sandy Insurance Company, incorporated in San Angelo, Texas, is
    A. an alien company in Illinois.
    B. a foreign company in Canada.
    C. a domestic company in Texas.
    D. a foreign company in Texas.

33. All of the following are purposes of the various state insurance departments EXCEPT to
    A. administer agent license exams.
    B. license companies to conduct business within the state.
    C. enact all laws pertaining to insurance matters within the state.
    D. regulate trade practices.

34. To make a sale, an agent assures a prospect that a policy will pay benefits for a type of loss that the policy excludes. This is an example of
    A. adequate disclosure.
    B. a disreputable, but not illegal, sales practice.
    C. an unfair claims settlement practice.
    D. misrepresentation.

35. An application for insurance is a
    A. form that outlines the insuring agreements.
    B. binder that guarantees the coverage requested.
    C. release to the company for application of a claim payment.
    D. written document containing information about the insured for use by the company.

36. Some insurance companies seek other insurance companies to share a portion of a given risk. They do this in accordance with the principle of
    A. reinsurance.
    B. indemnification.
    C. concurrency.
    D. apportionment.

37. The primary purpose of the insurance agent is to
    A. collect the premiums for the policy.
    B. act as the sales representative between the insurer and the insured.
    C. settle all claims submitted by the insured.
    D. type the policy for issue.

38. Grant, an agent, represents only the Direct City Insurance Company. He therefore could be referred to as a/an
    A. broker agent.
    B. general agent.
    C. nonexclusive agent.
    D. exclusive agent.

39. The person having the final authority concerning the acceptance or rejection of a risk is called the
    A. agent.
    B. adjuster.
    C. broker.
    D. underwriter.

40. The insurance company department that is concerned with interpreting state insurance law and making sure company policy forms and practices are in compliance would be the
    A. Actuarial Department.
    B. Agency Department.
    C. Legal Department.
    D. Policy Issue Department.

41. An insurance company employee who inspects losses and estimates indemnification would work in the
    A. Claim Department.
    B. Agency Department.
    C. Underwriting Department.
    D. Auditing Department.

42. An insurance company employee most concerned with the determination and establishment of rates would work in the
    A. Accounting Department.
    B. Agency Department.
    C. Actuarial Department.
    D. Underwriting Department.

43. The department within an insurance company most interested in loss prevention and assisting insureds with their safety program would be the
    A. Legal Department.
    B. Loss Control Department.
    C. Agency Department.
    D. Underwriting Department.

44. A factor that increases the chance that a loss will occur is called a
    A. peril.
    B. unit of exposure.
    C. hazard.
    D. risk.

45. An underwriter should always be aware of a moral hazard. This means that he or she
    A. is aware of those individuals whose lifestyle is more acceptable to the majority of Americans.
    B. sits in judgment of the personal actions of an individual.
    C. should be aware of those people who become more careless when they have insurance protection.
    D. must determine whether the individual would purposely create a loss to collect on the insurance.

46. What type of hazard is normally represented by a factory that handles hazardous chemicals?
    A. Moral
    B. Physical
    C. Morale
    D. Perilous

47. The premium for a unique risk would probably be determined using
    A. merit rating.
    B. manual rating.
    C. retrospective rating.
    D. judgment rating.

48. The formula for determining a premium is
    A. rate × exposure units = premium.
    B. rate = premium (they are the same).
    C. rate = premium × exposure units.
    D. exposure units − rate = premium.

49. Suppose Geraldine purchases a special insurance policy to protect her valuable fur coat. The agent says that the premium is actually $19, but the company must charge at least $25. This is an example of
    A. an earned premium.
    B. an unearned premium.
    C. a minimum premium.
    D. subrogation.

50. Suppose the Cheyenne Insurance Company issues a policy to Allen on January 15. Allen decides that after March 15 of the same year, he no longer requires coverage and wishes to cancel the policy. There will be approximately
    A. two months of earned premium involved.
    B. ten months of earned premium involved.
    C. two months of unearned premium involved.
    D. twelve months of earned premium involved.

51. Suppose Garrett, a rater with Coco Casualty Company, uses rates that are readily chosen from printed pages received at his office. This is an example of
    A. judgment rating.
    B. retrospective rating.
    C. experience rating.
    D. manual rating.

52. Which of the following methods involves the determination of premiums using a discount based on past experience?
    A. Manual rating
    B. Merit rating
    C. Reinsurance rating
    D. Judgment rating

53. Which statement best defines the insurance contract?
    A. A written agreement, by the insured, to pay money to the insurer
    B. A written agreement, by the insurer, to pay for all losses suffered by the insured
    C. A legally binding agreement, with consideration, between two parties
    D. A nonbinding agreement, between two parties, to provide payment of money to one party in case of loss

54. The consideration given by the insured in an insurance contract is the
    A. insurance policy.
    B. claims reimbursement.
    C. underwriting decision.
    D. premium.

55. Here is a sample part of an insurance policy: 'In consideration of payment of premium the company will indemnify the insured for all losses as a result of fire, windstorm, or theft.' This portion would be part of the
    A. exclusions.
    B. conditions.
    C. insuring agreement.
    D. declarations.

56. Here is a sample part of an insurance policy: 'This policy does not apply to any property damage incurred as a result of nuclear attack or the result of an explosion of any nuclear powered device.' This portion would be part of the
    A. declarations.
    B. conditions.
    C. insuring agreement.
    D. exclusions.

57. Here is a sample part of an insurance policy: 'In the event of loss, the named insured must report the loss within 60 days.' This portion would be part of the
    A. exclusions.
    B. conditions.
    C. declarations.
    D. insuring agreement.

58. Joe receives his policy from the Statue Insurance Company. A modification to it has been made by an attachment stapled to the policy. This is called a/an
    A. declaration.
    B. proof of loss notice.
    C. insurable interest.
    D. endorsement.

59. A type of policy issued by several different companies, but with identical wording, is called a
    A. standard policy.
    B. mutual policy.
    C. stock policy.
    D. reciprocal policy.

60. Which one of the following policies entitles the insured to receive dividends?
    A. Floater policy
    B. Participating policy
    C. Nonparticipating policy
    D. Valued policy

61. Suppose the following dates appear in the Declarations: 1/1/98–1/1/99. The period of time between these two dates is called the
    A. effective date.
    B. limit of insurance.
    C. policy period.
    D. expiration date.

62. The type of coverage that is written to cover property at one fixed location is called
    A. floater coverage.
    B. participating coverage.
    C. fixed coverage.
    D. reporting coverage.

63. Which one of the following policies sets forth a specific amount agreed upon to be payable in the event of a total loss?
    A. Nonparticipating policy
    B. Floater policy
    C. Participating policy
    D. Valued policy

64. Which of the following would be a package policy?
    A. Mary purchases one insurance policy to provide property coverage for her house and another to cover her personal liability exposures.
    B. Ralph purchases a policy that provides both property and liability coverage for his exposures as a homeowner.
    C. Henry purchases an insurance policy that provides property insurance for his house and a separate policy to protect his business property.
    D. Linda purchases a theft insurance policy for her personal property.

65. Which one of the following policies covers the described property at any location?
    A. Participating policy
    B. Valued policy
    C. Nonparticipating policy
    D. Floater policy

66. With a reporting policy, the insured
    A. pays a deposit premium and then provides periodic reports to the insurer so the premium can be adjusted.
    B. pays no premium until the end of the policy period.
    C. pays a set premium for each policy period.
    D. can collect dividends.

67. Easy-to-read insurance policies
    A. use highly technical language.
    B. feature clear language and larger type.
    C. are rare.
    D. are being replaced in most states by more legalistic documents.

68. Personal lines refers to insurance written for
    A. security risks.
    B. individuals or families.
    C. businesses.
    D. invasion of privacy risks.

69. Which one of the following is NOT a method used by insurers to determine the amount of indemnification for a loss?
    A. Actual cash value
    B. Market value
    C. Replacement cost
    D. Combined ratio

70. John's home is valued at $125,000. He has it insured under a policy with an 80% coinsurance requirement. If John carries $75,000 of coverage and suffers a $75,000 loss, how much will he collect?
    A. $56,250
    B. $125,000
    C. $75,000
    D. $0

71. If an insured obtains coverage by an intentional misrepresentation or concealment of a material fact, the insurance company could
    A. void the policy.
    B. suspend the policy.
    C. subrogate the policy.
    D. waive the policy.

72. Suppose the Acme Brick Company agrees to provide a night watchman at its plant. This fact is stated in the policy issued by the Allsweet Insurance Company. This is an example of a
    A. waiver in the policy.
    B. warranty in the policy.
    C. binder required of the company.
    D. participating policy.

73. Which party in an insurance contract may cancel a policy by notifying the other party in writing or surrendering the policy to the other party?
    A. The insured only
    B. Both the insured and the insurance company
    C. Neither the insured nor the insurance company
    D. The insurance company only

74. The cause of loss is a
    A. peril.
    B. condition.
    C. risk.
    D. hazard.

75. Suppose Burt receives a notice that his insurance policy is being renewed. This means that
    A. he will have to write the company asking them to cancel the former policy.
    B. his coverage is being extended for another period of time.
    C. he is now being issued a participating policy.
    D. his newly acquired automobile is now covered by the policy.

76. Suppose an insured purchases insurance to protect her home. Should damage from the peril of fire occur, the company has promised to repair the damage without deducting an amount for depreciation of the property. Which type of insurance protection does the insured have?
    A. Actual cash value
    B. Coinsurance
    C. Replacement cost coverage
    D. Deductible

77. Suppose an insured feels that a loss settlement offered by his insurance company is inadequate. He initiates appraisal action. His appraiser and the company's appraiser cannot agree on an amount, so an umpire is called in. The final determination of the amount the insured will be reimbursed occurs when
    A. the insurer and one appraiser agree to an amount.
    B. the insured and one appraiser agree to an amount.
    C. any two of the three parties (two appraisers and one umpire) agree to an amount.
    D. both appraisers and the umpire agree to an amount.

78. A property is valued at $80,000. The insurance contract has an 80% coinsurance clause. This means that the property owner
    A. will be paid only 80% of the total amount of the loss.
    B. must carry insurance protection to at least $64,000 on the property to be fully compensated under the contract up to the limit of insurance.
    C. should have insurance in the amount of $80,000 to then be paid 80% of any loss.
    D. must deduct 20% from the total amount of a loss as the insured's share of the loss.

79. A building is valued at $50,000. The owner has insurance to $40,000 to meet the requirement of an 80% coinsurance clause. The building suffers a $30,000 loss. The insurance company will pay
    A. $50,000.
    B. $24,000.
    C. $40,000.
    D. $30,000.

80. Carl has an accident. He notifies his agent, who will ask that he complete the form called a
    A. cash value of loss notice.
    B. binder.
    C. standard loss endorsement.
    D. proof of loss notice.

81. An individual borrows money from the Last National Bank to purchase a home. In this situation, the bank is the (mortgagee/mortgagor) _____ and it (does/does not) _____ hold an insurable interest in the home.
    A. mortgagee, does not
    B. mortgagor, does not
    C. mortgagor, does
    D. mortgagee, does

82. An insured has a policy that includes a deductible clause. This means that
    A. the insured must deduct the loss payment from the value of the policy.
    B. the insured must pay an amount, up to a certain specified limit, for each loss incurred under the applicable portion of the policy.
    C. any losses paid to a third party are deducted from the limits set forth in the Declarations portion of the policy.
    D. the insured deducts any payment received from the insurance premium.

83. When an insured suffers a loss to covered property, the insured should do all of the following EXCEPT
    A. mail the insurance policy to the company.
    B. complete a detailed proof of loss.
    C. notify the company.
    D. protect the property from further damage.

84. A policy that insures property only against the perils that are specifically listed in the policy is a/an
    A. specified perils policy.
    B. all risk policy.
    C. open perils policy.
    D. special coverage policy.

85. Four different companies each insure a building for a total amount of $40,000. The appraised value is $42,000. If each company has the same share of insurance coverage, how much would each pay in the event of a total loss settled on a pro rata basis?
    A. $10,000
    B. $30,000
    C. $40,000
    D. $20,000

86. Suppose Kyle is insured by Company A. He suffers a loss due to the negligence of Kim, insured by Company B. Company A pays Kyle for his loss. Company A may now
    A. recover payments from Company B due to the right of subrogation.
    B. sue Company B under the loss payee clause.
    C. assign the policy to Company B under the concurrency clause.
    D. exclude Company B from future business in that state under the apportionment clause.

87. Once an insured has received payment for a loss from his or her own insurance company, if the other party was at fault, the insured transfers the right of recovery for that loss to
    A. both companies involved.
    B. the other company involved.
    C. the other party involved in the accident.
    D. the insured's insurance company.

88. An assignment, as used in connection with insurance, is
    A. binding upon the insurance company with or without its consent.
    B. the assignment of certain rates to different risks.
    C. the transfer of interest in the policy from one party to another with the consent of the company.
    D. the assignment of modes of settlement by a company to the relatives of the deceased insured.

89. A Homeowners policy provides
    A. property, liability, and auto coverage.
    B. both property and liability coverage.
    C. liability coverage only.
    D. property coverage only.

90. Under a Homeowners contract, Medical Payments coverage is paid
    A. without regard to fault.
    B. only when liability has been established.
    C. only when the limit of insurance for Liability coverage has been used up.
    D. when the insured becomes ill.

91. An automobile policy used to insure the automobile exposures of individuals or families is the
    A. Personal Liability and Medical Payments to Others policy.
    B. Commercial Auto policy.
    C. Homeowners policy.
    D. Personal Auto policy.

92. Which coverage in the Personal Auto policy reimburses the insured for damage to the insured's own car?
    A. Physical Damage
    B. Liability
    C. Medical Payments
    D. Mechanical Breakdown

93. In general, damage caused to the insured's vehicle by impact with another vehicle or object is paid under which of the following specific Personal Auto policy coverages?
    A. Comprehensive
    B. Supplementary Payments
    C. Collision
    D. Specified Perils

94. Any of the following types of coverage can be provided as part of the Commercial Package Policy's Commercial Property coverage part EXCEPT
    A. Crime.
    B. Business Income and Extra Expense.
    C. Builders Risk.
    D. Building and Personal Property.

95. Which one of the following exposures is NOT covered under the Commercial General Liability coverage part of the CPP?
    A. Products liability
    B. Premises and operations liability
    C. Professional liability
    D. Completed operations liability

96. Workers' compensation insurance
    A. provides retirement benefits for employees.
    B. provides disability benefits for employees injured off the job.
    C. covers an employer for benefits the employer must pay under state law to employees injured on the job.
    D. covers an employer's loss of income when workers go on strike.

97. The extra effort insurers have made to respond effectively to catastrophes such as Hurricane Andrew, the California earthquakes, the Northeastern blizzard, and the Midwest floods is an example of promoting better understanding of insurance through
    A. seeking publicity.
    B. stricter regulatory compliance.
    C. extensive advertising.
    D. improving service.

98. All of the following are reasons that insurance is not like gambling EXCEPT
    A. insurance covers only pure risks.
    B. there is no financial gain in insurance, even if insureds receive more on a claim than they paid in premiums—benefits simply restore insureds to the approximate financial condition they were in before a loss.
    C. insurance has nothing to do with risk.
    D. insurance operates by the principle of indemnity, but gambling doesn't.

99. What value do insureds receive for purchasing insurance if they never have a claim?
    A. Nothing
    B. A larger share in the profits of the company than insureds who have filed claims
    C. The peace of mind of having coverage—being able to exchange the uncertainty of a burdensome financial loss for a smaller, known cost
    D. A return of all their premiums at the end of the policy period

100. The factor that accounts for an insurance company's largest outflow of money by far is
    A. paying insureds' losses and loss adjustment expenses.
    B. return of unearned premium on policies canceled before their expiration date.
    C. transaction fees on buying and selling investments.
    D. general operating expenses.

ANSWERS AND RATIONALES

1. **B.** People who buy insurance benefit in terms of financial stability by getting help in recovering from losses.

2. **B.** People can benefit from insurance even if they don't own it themselves. If this business had been insured, it could have been rebuilt quickly, allowing employees to get back to work and the flow of economic activity from that business to resume.

3. **A.** The benefits of insurance flow to virtually everyone, not only to those who own it.

4. **C.** Everyone who is involved in the insurance industry has an impact on the service that insureds ultimately receive. Every loss or concern of an insured deserves a prompt and caring response.

5. **A.** Ben Franklin not only organized the first U.S. fire insurer, but also reduced fire losses by educating the public on fire hazards, inventing the lightning rod and the Franklin stove, and organizing Philadelphia's first volunteer fire department. Since that time, insurers have promoted safety and reduced the incidence of fires, crime, and other losses through advertising, legislative lobbying, and employment of loss control specialists and engineers.

6. **A.** This illustrates how insurance helps people obtain credit. The bank is more willing to extend credit because its financial interest in the property is protected by insurance.

7. **B.** The insurance industry is a major employer, taxpayer, and investor. These activities contribute to the nation's economic well-being.

8. **C.** People who buy insurance gain some very valuable benefits in terms of financial stability and in the form of help in recovering from and preventing losses and in obtaining credit.

9. **A.** In insurance terminology, 'premium' refers to the cost the insured pays for the coverage that is provided by an insurance policy.

10. **A.** Affordable cost is one of the elements of insurability. This means that the cost should be a fraction of the value. Fire insurance meets this requirement because, as an example, a homeowner might pay $400 for $100,000 of coverage.

11. **C.** Insurance exchanges the uncertainty of loss for the certainty of coverage. Not every loss is paid, and if a loss does not occur, the insured will not receive any money back. Insurance does not ensure that property remains in good condition, nor is it a type of savings plan.

12. **D.** Insurance companies use the law of large numbers to predict their losses.

13. **A.** Insurance is a device that allows the losses that occur to a relatively small number of people to be shared among the members of a large group. A peril is the cause of a loss. A hazard is something that increases the chance of a loss.

14. **D.** One of the principles of insurability is that a loss must be accidental in nature (i.e., unexpected and beyond the insured's control).

15. **C.** The opposite is true; one of the elements of insurability is that losses do not normally occur to large numbers of people at the same time.

16. **A.** While a risk can be avoided, it can't be rejected altogether.

17. **B.** Pure risks are insurable; speculative risks are not.

18. **B.** A basic tenet of insurance is that a person must have an insurable interest, or a financial interest that poses the possibility of financial loss, before he or she can purchase insurance.

19. **B.** Indemnification means the insured will receive a payment that restores him or her to the same financial position that he or she occupied before the loss—no more and no less.

20. **A.** A joint insurable interest arises when two or more parties stand to lose financially if a loss occurs.

21. **C.** Casualty insurance includes a wide variety of coverages, one of the most important of which is liability insurance. Health and disability insurance handles the risks of incurring medical expenses or not being able to earn a living after getting sick or injured. Property insurance covers losses to an individual's personal property.

22. **B.** Liability for damage to another's property is a casualty loss, not a property loss.

23. **B.** Although liability is one of the most important casualty lines, many other types of insurance, including some property types, have traditionally been included as casualty coverages. Some examples are glass, aviation, auto, boiler and machinery, crime, workers' compensation, and fidelity and surety bonds.

24. **A.** Negligence is the failure to use proper care in personal actions.

25. **A.** The losses involving the furnace explosion and lightning damage are property losses. The situation where the insured was involved in a car accident represents a liability loss for the other driver, not the insured.

26. **B.** Negligence is an important concept that can determine whether or not a person is legally liable for actions that cause harm to others.

27. **C.** Although it may be possible for stockholders to purchase policies from the company or for policyholders to purchase stock, in a stock insurance company, the owners and the customers are generally two separate parties.

28. **D.** A mutual company is owned by its policyholders.

29. **A.** Under a reciprocal arrangement, all members essentially insure each other and share the losses. In a mutual company, the policyholders own the company. In a stock company, policyholders are not necessarily stockholders; stock dividends are paid to the stockholders rather than to the policyholders. A Lloyd's association is a syndicate of private insurers who voluntarily agree to write coverage for a variety of risks.

30. **C.** A Lloyd's association is a syndicate of private individuals or groups of individuals who voluntarily agree to issue insurance.

31. **B.** A domestic company is one that is doing business in the state in which it is domiciled. An alien company is one that is domiciled in another country but doing business in a certain state. An admitted insurer is one authorized to sell insurance in a particular state. A nonadmitted insurer is exactly the opposite—one that is NOT authorized to write insurance in a certain state.

32. **C.** It would be considered a foreign company while operating in any other state but Texas and an alien company while operating in a country outside the United States.

33. **C.** State legislatures develop and pass insurance laws.

34. **D.** Agents must accurately describe policy features, terms, and benefits. To do otherwise is a deceptive sales practice that violates the law.

35. **D.** The application contains a description of the prospect and the risk to be covered and is signed by the prospect. The company uses

this information to decide whether to issue coverage and, if so, the appropriate premium to charge.

36. **A.** Reinsurance with other companies permits an insurer to accept larger risks than it would otherwise be able to write.

37. **B.** While agents may collect premiums, this is not their primary purpose. Agents do not settle claims or type policies for issue.

38. **D.** An exclusive agent represents only one insurance company.

39. **D.** The purpose of an Underwriting Department is to make certain the company's standards and goals are met by accepting only those risks that are acceptable to that particular company. Underwriters also have other responsibilities that are designed to continuously check whether the company is accomplishing its goals through the risks it accepts.

40. **C.** Since insurance policies are legal contracts, it is important that such a department exist to make certain state insurance laws and any other regulations are followed in the practice of the business.

41. **A.** A claim representative works with insureds and third-party claimants to settle claims.

42. **C.** Actuaries are specialists in the mathematical formulas and statistics that relate to insurance rates and premiums.

43. **B.** The Loss Control Department inspects buildings and equipment and makes recommendations about how the risk of loss can be avoided or reduced. In addition, after a loss, this same department may become involved in determining the cause of a loss.

44. **C.** A peril is the cause of loss. A unit of exposure is a component in the manual rating formula. A risk is the chance of loss.

45. **D.** A moral hazard refers to a situation in which there is the possibility someone would intentionally create a loss situation in order to collect from an insurance company.

46. **B.** A physical hazard is one that arises from the condition, occupancy, or use of property. An occupancy that involves the use of hazardous chemicals would pose a physical hazard by increasing the chance of loss.

47. **D.** With judgment rating, a premium is determined based on an individual evaluation of the risk. No books or tables are used.

48. **A.** This is the basic formula used to establish the premium in manual rating.

49. **C.** On some policies with low premiums, it might cost the company more to issue the policy than it would receive in premium. For this reason, minimum premiums are established and used when the actual premium falls below the minimum.

50. **A.** Earned premium is that which the insurer actually has earned by virtue of having provided insurance coverage during a certain period. Since this policy was in force for two months, there were two months of earned premium.

51. **D.** With manual rating, insurance companies group insureds by class according to certain common risk characteristics. Rates are based on actual loss experience for insureds in each class. The rates for each class are contained in a manual (or stored on a computer) and used to calculate the premium for each insured.

52. **B.** Generally, the merit rating calculation begins with a premium that is derived by manual rating, and then a discount or a surcharge is applied to the premium to account for past loss experience.

53. **C.** A workable definition is "a legal agreement between two parties for consideration."

54. **D.** The consideration that the insurer gives is the promise to pay for certain losses suffered by the insured.

55. **C.** The insuring agreement states in general what a policy will cover—the perils of fire, windstorm, or theft in this case.

56. **D.** The exclusions section describes the losses the policy does not cover. If an excluded loss occurs, the insurer will not indemnify the insured.

57. **B.** The conditions state the policy's ground rules by describing the responsibilities of both the insurance company and the insured.

58. **D.** Anytime a policy is modified from the original version, a written endorsement must be attached to the policy indicating that both the insured and the company have agreed to the modification.

59. **A.** Certain policies have been standardized by law and insuring organizations such as the ISO. Court interpretations through the years have also resulted in companies using wording that has already been interpreted, leaving little doubt about what a policy actually covers. This standard wording helps companies avoid the legal pitfalls that can arise with untested wording.

60. **B.** Under a participating policy, the insured receives a dividend if claims and other expenses during the year do not exceed the cost of the insurance. There is no similar dividend for the insured under a nonparticipating policy. A floater policy covers property at any location, not just a single fixed location. A valued policy is one that specifies a certain amount of insurance is to be paid in the event of a total loss.

61. **C.** The policy period begins on the policy's effective date (the time and date coverage under the policy goes into effect) and ends on the expiration date (the time and date coverage under the policy expires). The limit of insurance represents the maximum dollar amount the insurer will pay for a loss.

62. **C.** An example of fixed coverage is fire insurance on a house.

63. **D.** Valued policies are often used for properties whose values can be difficult to determine, such as antiques or stamp collections. A participating policy is one that provides dividends for insureds if claims and other expenses during the year do not exceed the cost of the insurance. There is no similar dividend for the insured under a nonparticipating policy. A floater policy covers property at any location, not just a single fixed location.

64. **B.** A package policy is one that includes two or more types of coverage in a single policy. Ralph's single policy provides two different types of coverages.

65. **D.** Floater coverage is designed to protect property that moves around, such as a car.

66. **A.** Policies are issued on a reporting basis when it is difficult to determine in advance what amount of coverage should be purchased.

67. **B.** Early insurance policies used very technical, legal language that was difficult for an insured to understand. Easy-to-read policies replaced this legalese with language that is more direct and easier to understand.

68. **B.** Insurance designed for businesses is called commercial lines.

69. **D.** The combined ratio measures the extent to which premium income covers a company's losses and expenses.

70. **A.** John doesn't carry enough insurance to meet the coinsurance requirement, so he will not be paid the full amount of the loss. In this case, the loss payment is calculated by dividing the amount of insurance carried by the amount of insurance required and then multiplying this figure by the amount of loss.

71. **A.** Since an insurance company relies on the insured to not misrepresent or conceal anything material to issuing the policy, misrepresentation or concealment is grounds for the company to void the policy.

72. **B.** A warranty is simply a promise by one party to do something or not to do something. If the insured makes a warranty and then fails to keep it, the company is justified in denying coverage in the event of loss, according to court rulings.

73. **A.** While there is only one acceptable way for the insurance company to cancel a policy—notifying the insured in writing—the insured has the option of notifying the company in writing or surrendering the policy to the company.

74. **A.** A risk is a chance of loss. A hazard is something that increases the possibility of loss. A condition is something in an insurance policy that describes the duties and responsibilities of the insured or the insurer.

75. **B.** Renewal is the continuation of an insurance contract beyond the original date of expiration.

76. **C.** Replacement cost coverage means the company will pay whatever it costs to replace the property without regard to depreciation. This coverage is generally subject to some conditions the insured is required to meet in order to qualify.

77. **C.** The appraisal condition says that both parties can obtain the service of an appraiser. If the appraisers cannot agree on an amount, they submit their differences to an umpire. The decision agreed to by any two of the three is the final amount of indemnification.

78. **B.** A policy with an 80% coinsurance clause requires an insured to insure the property for at least 80% of its value, or $64,000 in this case.

79. **D.** Since the insured has met the coinsurance requirement, the full amount of loss will be paid, without deduction for depreciation.

80. **D.** A proof of loss notice both advises the company that a loss has occurred and provides an official inventory of the damages.

81. **D.** The lienholder is the mortgagee; the person who owns the home on which there is a lien is the mortgagor. The mortgagee has an insurable interest in the property until the lien is paid off.

82. **B.** To reduce the cost of insurance, companies use a deductible amount, which means that the insured pays the first dollar amount of any loss up to the amount of the deductible.

83. **A.** The duties following loss clause describes what insureds must do when a loss occurs. The insured would not have to mail the policy to the company because the insurer would already have a copy.

84. **A.** An open perils policy does not list specific perils; it insures against all perils that are not specifically excluded by the policy. 'All risk' and 'special coverage' are alternate terms for open perils policies.

85. **A.** Since the amount of insurance is divided equally among the four insurers, each insurer would pay 25% of the loss, or $10,000.

86. **A.** Subrogation is the substitution of one person (the insurance company) in the place of another (the insured) with regard to a lawful claim, demand, or right.

87. **D.** This is called subrogation. The insured's company is now entitled to any rights of recovery the insured has against the other party since the insurer has made payment. The insured's company can now try to recoup its payment from the party who was at fault.

88. **C.** An assignment is desirable when ownership of property passes from the insured to another party. However, because the insurance company has the right to know to whom it issues insurance coverage, it has the right to approve or disapprove of the assignment.

89. **B.** A Homeowners policy contains both property and liability coverages. It cannot be used to insure autos.

90. **A.** Medical Payments coverage pays for medical bills that are incurred by people who are injured on the insured's property or as a result of the insured's personal activities, regardless of whether the insured is legally at fault.

91. **D.** The Commercial Auto policy covers autos a business owns, borrows, rents, leases, or hires. The Homeowners policy does not cover autos. There is no such thing as a Personal Liability and Medical Payments to Others policy.

92. **A.** Liability coverage covers the insured's legal liability for bodily injury or property damage that arises out of the ownership, use, or maintenance of autos. Medical Payments coverage pays for medical bills and funeral expenses if the insured or his or her family members are struck by an auto or injured in an auto accident. There is no mechanical breakdown coverage in the Personal Auto policy.

93. **C.** Part D—Coverage for Damage to Your Auto provides two basic coverages. Collision coverage protects against damage that results from the insured auto's impact with another vehicle or object or the upset of the auto. Comprehensive coverage pays for just about every other type of auto physical damage loss except collision.

94. **A.** Crime insurance is a separate line that requires its own coverage part.

95. **C.** Professional liability must be insured under specialized malpractice or errors and omissions policies.

96. **C.** From workers' compensation laws arose the need for workers' compensation insurance to provide businesses with coverage for amounts they might be required by law to pay injured employees.

97. **D.** The insurance industry has improved its service to make itself and its product better understood.

98. **C.** With insurance, if a loss occurs, an insured doesn't gain anything. The insured is simply restored to the same financial condition he or she enjoyed prior to the loss.

99. **C.** Insureds who don't have claims still use their insurance—to obtain credit to buy a home or to meet the financial requirements of driving a car, for example.

100. **A.** For every dollar in premium collected, investment earnings add about 15 cents to insurance company income. Out of that total amount, about 80 cents is paid out in claims and claim expenses.

Glossary

A

Abandonment Surrender to the insurer of all interest in insured property after an event insured against has occurred. Not permitted under most property insurance contracts. Applies to property, or physical damage coverages, in Fire, Marine and Auto Insurance.

Accident A sudden unexpected event, identifiable in time and place. In some policies, the definition of accident has been broadened to mean the same as *occurrence*.

Accident and Health A type of insurance that protects against loss resulting from personal accident or sickness. It is written by both casualty and life companies.

Accounts Current A statement furnished monthly to agents showing all business written and canceled during the previous month. Used by agents to remit the premiums due the company, less commissions.

Act of God An event that is caused by the forces of nature, without human intervention, and that could not have been prevented by reasonable care, e.g., flood, lightning, earthquake, hurricane, etc.

Actual Cash Value An amount which limits the company's payment to the actual cash value of an item at the time of loss or damage. Usually includes a deduction for depreciation.

Actuary A technical expert on insurance, particularly versed in the mathematics of insurance, including the calculation of premiums, policy reserves and other values.

Adjuster A person, usually a salaried employee, who settles or adjusts claims.

Adjustment The process of determining the amount of a loss followed by settlement of the claim.

Admitted Company (or Insurer) An insurer licensed under the law of a state to do business in that state.

Advance Premium A deposit premium paid by the insured which may later be adjusted up or down, following an audit of the insured's records (i.e., payroll, inventory, sales receipts).

Agency Department An insurance company department in charge of agents and agencies. The agency department is responsible for supervising of agents.

Agent A person who represents the company and sells insurance on a commission basis. May be an "exclusive" or "nonexclusive" agent.

Agent, Exclusive An agent of a specific insurance company with the responsibility for selling insurance. Usually paid by commission. Represents only one company.

Agent, Nonexclusive An agent in business for himself or herself, selling insurance for many different companies. Paid by commission on sales.

Alien Company A company whose home office or domicile is located in a foreign country.

Annual Statement The company's yearly financial report to insurance departments issued at the close of the year. This report is required by the various insurance departments and is made according to a form agreed upon by the supervising authorities.

App A short term for application which is an order received from an agent for the writing of a policy.

Applicant A person who fills out and signs a written application for insurance.

Application A questionnaire providing space for information to be used to determine the insurance coverage required, as well as the acceptability of the insurance risk and the amount of premium. A questionnaire which must be filled in, when required, by the person seeking insurance. It gives the company full information about the proposed subject of insurance and the person to be insured, for the purpose of determining whether the company will issue the policy. In some types of insurance, it becomes part of the policy.

Apportionment Where more than one insurance contract covers a loss, the determination of extent to which each contract covers.

Appraisal Determination of the value of property, or of the extent of damage, usually by impartial experts. Provided for by a clause in some types of insurance contracts.

Appreciation Rise in value or price. Increase in worth or value.

Arbitration Clause Clause of policy that provides for mediation to resolve areas of disagreement between the insured and the insurance company, the insurance company and a third party in the case of liability insurance, or two or more insurance companies when other insurance is involved.

Arson The willful and malicious burning of property, sometimes with the intent of defrauding insurance companies.

Assigned Risk A driver or owner who cannot qualify for insurance in the regular market. This driver must get coverage through a state assigned risk plan which specifies that each company must accept a proportionate share of poor risk applicants. Premiums are usually higher and coverage is restricted.

Assignment The transfer of one's interest in an insurance contract to another; in many kinds of insurance, valid only with the consent of the insurer; the transfer, after an event insured against, of one's right to collect an amount payable under an insurance contract.

Assured Synonym for insured (i.e., one who has insurance). Specifically, one who has an insurance policy; a policyholder. The term is outdated. Insured is the preferred term.

Attorney-In-Fact An individual who is given the power of transacting stated kinds of business for another by a written contract, called a *power of attorney*. Used most often in insurance to define the powers of the person who operates a "reciprocal exchange" or "interinsurance exchange."

Attractive Nuisance A dangerous place or instrumentality attractive to children. The owner of an "attractive nuisance" has the legal duty of taking unusual care to guard children from it.

Authorized Insurer An insurer approved by the state or legally allowed to transact business in the state for the types of insurance for which they may be licensed.

B

Bailee One who has custody of the property of another. Bailees "for hire" have certain responsibilities to care for the property of others.

Basic Limits Certain minimum amounts of liability to be covered by insurance. It is customary to quote premiums in terms of these minimum amounts.

Binder Notification from an agent that insurance has been effected and is immediately in force; used in certain cases to protect a policyholder when it is not possible to issue a policy or endorse the old policy immediately. A temporary agreement that the policy is in effect.

Bodily Injury Injury to the body of a person. The term is usually specifically defined in the policy, and these individual definitions have variations.

Broker A term generally used to describe one who places business with more than one company, and who has no exclusive contract requiring that all business first be offered to a single company. Unlike the agent, who is considered to represent a company, the broker usually is considered to represent the insured.

Budget Payments A method of paying premiums by installments.

C

Cancellation Termination of an insurance contract before the end of the policy period, by the insured or insurer, usually in accordance with provisions in the contract.

    Flat Cancellation of an insurance contract as of its date of inception, without premium charge.

    Pro Rata Termination of an insurance contract or bond, with the premium charge then adjusted in proportion to the exact time the protection has been in force.

    Short-Rate Cancellation of an insurance contract at the request of the insured, with return to the insured of less than the proportion of the premium that is payable upon pro rata cancellation.

Captive Agent *See* Agent, Exclusive.

Career Agent *See* Agent, Exclusive.

Carrier An insurance company, or, in transportation insurance, a railroad, trucker or other transporter of goods.

Catastrophe An event which causes a loss of extraordinarily large values.

Claim A demand by an individual or corporation to recover under a policy of insurance for loss arising out of events covered by the policy. Claims are referred to the insurance company for handling on behalf of the insured in accordance with the contract terms. A demand for payment under an insurance contract or bond. The estimated or actual amount of a loss.

Claimant One who makes a claim.

Client The customer. The person who buys the insurance.

Code A number assigned to represent some characteristic of a risk. Shown on the daily report and the basis of most statistical work, e.g., a number for each state, a number for each occupancy class, a number for type of policy, etc.

Coinsurance A clause contained in some fire and burglary policies, requiring the insured to carry insurance equal to a stated percentage of the value of the insured property in order to collect the losses in full, up to the limits of the policy.

Coinsurer An insured or insurer that shares losses under a coinsurance arrangement.

Combined Ratio A measure of the extent to which premium income covers a company's losses and expenses, determined by adding together a company's loss ratio and its expense ratio.

Commercial Lines Insurance designed for businesses, institutions, or organizations.

Commission A percentage of the premium paid to an agent or broker in return for business procured by the agent.

Concealment Withholding of material facts from the insurer in negotiating an insurance contract or in making a claim.

Concurrent Insurance under two or more contracts, all the terms of which are identical, except that they may vary in amount or policy dates.

Conditions That portion of the insurance contract which outlines the duties and responsibilities of both the insured and the insurer.

Consequential Loss *See* Indirect Loss.

Consideration In an insurance contract, usually means money. The *premium* paid by the policyholder for the insurance protection.

Contract A legal agreement between two parties, for consideration. Insurance policies are contracts.

Contributory Negligence The act or omission to act on the part of one person, which, when taken with the act or omission of another, sometimes called a tortfeasor, can be considered a contributing cause of the accident or injury complained of.

Corrections The act of changing a policy by endorsement, adding or canceling coverages, or changing the policy terms.

Countersignature The signature of the insurer's representative which is usually required to validate an insurance policy.

Cover An insurance contract.

Coverage The guarantee against specific losses provided under the terms of a policy of insurance. Coverage is frequently used interchangeably with the word "protection." It is used synonymously with the word "insurance."

Credit Report A report obtained from a professional reporting company on the financial, physical and moral status of an insured or applicant.

D

Declarations Page That portion of the insurance contract which contains such information as: name and address of the insured, description of the property, coverage and premium amounts.

Deductible A certain dollar amount, specified in some property insurance policies, beyond which insurance protection begins. The insured assumes the loss up to the limit of the deductible amount; then the company pays any loss over that amount.

Direct Loss Loss that is the direct result of a peril. Compare to Indirect Loss.

Direct Response A marketing method that involves no agents. Insurance is sold directly to the public by soliciting responses by mail or other form of advertisement. Also, a company that uses this method of marketing.

Direct Writer An agent who represents only one company, or a company that employs such agents. *See* also Agent, Exclusive.

Disability Inability to carry on one's normal occupation due to personal injury or illness.

Disability Income A health insurance coverage which pays a specified monthly benefit in the event the insured is unable to work due to injury or illness.

Dividend A dividend on insurance contracts is the refund of that part of the premium paid at the beginning of the year which still remains after the company has set aside the necessary reserve and made deductions for claims and expenses. The dividend may also include a share in the company's investment, mortality and operating profits.

Domestic Insurer This term is used to describe an insurer within its state of domicile.

Draft An instrument having the external characteristics of a check, but differing in that the bank is authorized to transfer check funds on presentation of the instrument. They may transfer draft funds only when the draft has been accepted by the drawer and acknowledged by acceptance of the instrument as valid.

E

Earned Premium That portion of the premium which represents coverage already provided. Each day that an insurance policy is in force would be a day of earned premium.

Effective Date The starting date of a policy; the time at which the insurance protection begins.

Employers Liability A policy that covers employers who may be liable if, through their negligence, employees have been injured. Workers' Compensation pays the worker whether the employer has been negligent or not. Injury must be incurred in the course of employment.

Endorsement An amendment in writing (including printing or stamping) added to and made a part of the insurance contract for the purpose of changing the original terms—either to restrict or expand coverage.

Excess Insurance Insurance coverage above a specified amount; insurance coverage after the loss exceeds the amount of other insurance.

Exclusion Something not covered by the policy and specifically so stated in the policy contract.

Exclusions That portion of the insurance contract which specifies the losses *not* protected by the policy.

Expense Ratio A measure of a company's expenses, determined by dividing the company's expenses by its written premiums.

Experience A record of premiums and losses; the basis upon which future rates are predicted.

Expiration The date on which the insurance protection on a policy will end, e.g., coverage will cease on an annual policy at the end of 12 months from the effective date.

Expiration Notice A form sent to an agency (by the company) or to a named insured (by the agency) indicating that a policy is due to expire on a certain date. The form is often returned as an order for renewal of the policy.

F

Face Amount The total amount or principal amount of insurance provided by an insurance policy. The term derives from the fact that the amount of insurance is usually indicated on the first page or "face" of the policy.

Face Sheet A transcript of the daily report which shows the coverages carried by the insured, statistical coding and record of a claim.

Fidelity and Surety Bonds Insurance against dishonesty of employees. Guarantees the faithful administration of assets or the proper performance of contracts.

Field Representative Or Field Manager An employee who travels a given territory and calls on agents in the interest of the company. Sometimes called a Special Agent or Sales Manager.

Flat Cancellation Cancellation of a policy at or before it becomes effective with all the premium refunded to the policyholder.

Fleet Policy A policy which provides insurance for a number of vehicles owned by one insured; or, in marine insurance, a number of ships of one owner.

Floater Policy A policy under the terms of which protection follows movable property, covering it wherever it may be; for example, a policy on tourist's luggage.

Foreign Insurer This term is used to describe an insurer domiciled in another state.

Fraternal Organization A society or order operated for the benefit of its members and their beneficiaries, not for profit.

Fraud Deception or artifice used to deceive or cheat. In insurance it is understood to be related to misrepresentation and concealment. Proof of willful fraud is grounds for voiding a policy.

Furniture and Fixtures The contents of a building, excluding merchandise for sale or in the course of manufacture (stock) and machinery. Fixtures are attached to the building.

G

General Agent An agent who supervises other agents in a given territory and acts as an exclusive agent in this territory.

Glass Insurance Coverage for damage to glass caused by breakage or by chemicals accidentally or maliciously applied.

Grace Period The period of time, following the due date of the policy premium, during which the payment of the premium will continue the policy in force and during which the policy is in full force and effect. The length of the grace period varies with several factors.

Guest Laws State legislated provisions that the right of action of an injured guest passenger against the driver of an automobile is subject to proof that the driver was guilty of "willful and wanton" negligence. Apart from such laws, the guest passenger would have the same rights as any other member of the public and only be required to prove "ordinary" negligence. Not all states have "guest laws."

H

Hazard Anything that increases the chance of loss.

Hired Car Coverage Insurance protection for the insured against liability incurred while using automobiles hired from another firm or organization. The auto may be driven by an employee or a hired driver.

I

Incurred Losses Losses or claims which the company has paid or for which it has become liable; or paid losses plus reserves for a certain period, minus unpaid reserves at the end of the previous period.

Indemnification A principle of insurance which states that the individual should be restored to the approximate financial position occupied prior to the loss.

Indemnity, Principle Of Replacement, repair, or payment of value of a loss; to return the person to be indemnified to the financial condition which existed before the loss. Not to be confused with legal damages, which frequently go beyond indemnity.

Independent Adjuster One who adjusts losses on behalf of companies but is not on their payroll. The independent adjuster is paid by fee for each loss adjusted, as distinguished from a company adjuster who is paid a regular salary by one company.

Independent Agent An agent who represents more than one company.

Indirect Loss Loss that is a result or consequence of a direct loss.

Inland Marine A class of insurance developed from ocean cargo heritage. Covers property which is mobile in nature. Policies include transit hazards and generally provide "open perils" coverage. Examples: personal property floaters, contractors equipment, bailees' customers.

Inspection The investigation of certain risks which may be made by independent inspection firms or by the company before issuance or during the term of the policy.

Installment Premium One of several payments made by an insured until the entire policy premium is paid in full.

In Suit Claims involved in a law suit filed by a claimant against the insured.

Insurability, Requirements For Insurance theory states that before something is insurable it must meet the following requirements:

1. There must be sufficient numbers of people involved.
2. It must be a definite loss.
3. Loss must be accidental.
4. Potential loss must be large.
5. Cost of the insurance must be "affordable."

6. Loss must be calculable.
7. Loss must not be catastrophic.
8. Risk must be a pure risk.

Insurable Interest Relationship or condition such that loss or destruction of life or property would cause a financial loss. In the case of property insurance, such interest must exist at the time of the loss.

Insurance A social device where many share the losses of a few by transferring a portion of the loss to the insurance company in exchange for a certain cost.

Insurance Services Office (ISO) An organization established for the benefit of its member insurance companies and other subscriber companies. ISO gathers statistics, provides loss costs, drafts policy forms and coverage provisions, and conducts inspections for rate-making purposes.

Insured The person purchasing the insurance policy from the insurance company.

Insurer The insurance company. The one who issues the insurance policy.

Insuring Agreements That portion of the insurance contract which states those perils insured against—the coverage afforded by the policy.

Investigation The adjuster's activity in checking the manner in which damage occurred, securing the facts in connection with an accident, checking cars or other property damaged.

J

Joint Insurable Interest Two or more parties with a financial interest in a particular item of property.

Judgment Rating One of the oldest forms of determining rates. The rate is determined without the benefit of extensive loss experience or statistical information. The best judgment of the rater is used to set the cost of the insurance.

L

Law of Large Numbers The theory of probability that is the basis of insurance: the larger the number of risks or exposures, the more closely will the actual results obtained approach the probable results that would be expected from an infinite number of exposures.

Legal Liability Liability imposed by law, as opposed to liability arising from an agreement or contract.

Liability Insurance Insurance which agrees to pay on behalf of the policyholder sums the insured becomes legally required to pay to others as the result of negligence. May cover bodily injury to another or damage to property of another or both.

Liability Losses Losses an individual might suffer as a result of negligence which results in damage to the property of others. Damage for which the individual is legally liable.

License, Agents Certification, issued by a state department of insurance, that an individual is qualified to solicit insurance applications for the period covered. Usually issued for a period of one year, it is renewable on application without necessity of the individual's periodic repetition of the original qualifying requirements. Each agent should study carefully the licensing laws and regulations of the state in which the agent does business.

Lloyd's Association A voluntary association of individuals or groups of individuals who agree to share in insurance contracts. Each individual or "syndicate" is individually responsible for the amounts of insurance it writes.

Loss In insurance it means the amount the insurer is required to pay because of a happening against which it has insured. A *happening* that causes the company to pay. Also refers to the overall financial result of some operation, as opposed to "profit." The basis for a claim for indemnity or damage under terms of an insurance policy. Any diminution of the quality, quantity, or value of property.

Loss Control Specialist/Engineer Persons trained in safety work who call on the insurance purchaser to make corrective recommendations that may help to avoid injury to employees of the insured or to the general public. Also called loss control personnel.

Loss Costs The amount of money required for the insurance company to cover its losses, not including expenses of operation.

Loss Ratio A comparison of incurred losses and earned premiums obtained by dividing the earned premiums into the incurred losses.

M

Manual A publication containing underwriting rules, classification, and premium rates for a given type of insurance. May be contained in a computer rather than on printed pages.

Manual Rates Refers to the cost of insurance protection as quoted in the rating manual. It may also refer to those rates developed by the application of a recognized rating plan.

Manual Rating A method for determining the cost of an insurance policy using predetermined rates, usually obtained from a rate book or manual.

Medical Payments A coverage, written in connection with auto insurance, which provides medical expenses for the insured, family members and passengers when they are injured accidentally from riding in a car covered by the insured's policy or for the insured and family members when struck by an auto. In case of death from such injury, funeral expenses may be included.

Merit Rating A method for determining the future cost of an insurance policy by charging an amount based upon past experience for that risk.

Minimum Premium The lowest amount of premium required to issue certain policies. Anything less than the minimum would not even cover the company's expense of handling the policy.

Misrepresentation To make written or verbal statements that are untrue or misleading, either on the part of the applicant in describing the risk or, on the part of an insurer or agent, regarding the policy terms.

Monoline Policy An insurance policy that includes coverage from one line of insurance.

Moral Hazard The hazard present in an insuring situation if the insured purposely creates a loss to then collect from the insurance company.

Morale Hazard The hazard present in an insuring situation if the insured, through carelessness or as a result of his or her own irresponsible actions, creates a loss.

Mortgagee The party loaning money toward the purchase of personal property. Most commonly, a bank or other loaning institution.

Mortgagee Clause A clause in an insurance contract making the proceeds payable to a named mortgagee, as interest may appear, and stating the terms of the contract between the insurer and the mortgagee.

Mortgagor The party borrowing money to purchase property.

Mutual Company One which has no capital stock, is owned by the policyholders, is managed by a board of directors chosen by the policyholders, and usually issues participating insurance only.

N

Named Insured The person designated in the policy as the insured as opposed to someone who may have an interest in a policy, but is not named in it. Usually includes a spouse if a resident of the same household.

Named Peril Insurance policy that insures only against perils named in the policy. Also called a specified peril policy.

Negligence Failure to do what a reasonably prudent individual would ordinarily do under the circumstances of a particular case, or doing what a prudent person would not have done. Negligence may be caused by acts of omission, commission, or both.

No-Fault Insurance Any insurance coverage in which individuals are indemnified for their own losses by their insurance company, regardless of fault. Most frequently refers to coverage for an insured's medical expenses in states with no-fault laws.

Nonadmitted Insurer An insurer not authorized to do business in a given state.

Nonownership Automobile Liability A coverage protecting the insured against liability incurred by employees while driving an automobile not owned or hired by the policyholder. Usually the employee is driving his or her own car on business for the insured.

Nonparticipating Policy A type of policy which does *not* return to the insured the excess premium over the amount required for losses or other expenses incurred in the issue of the policy. Normally issued by stock companies.

Not Taken A policy that has been issued but not accepted by the insured and, therefore, is canceled.

O

Occupational Disease Coverage A coverage which pays benefits for diseases arising out of or in the course of employment, as opposed to ordinary diseases to which the general public is exposed.

Occurrence Coverage on an "occurrence" basis is generally considered to differ from coverage on an "accident" basis in that "occurrence" connotes gradual or accumulative damage without regard to exact time or place, whereas "accident" refers to instantaneous damage, identifiable as to time and place. In other words, "occurrence" may be defined as an event, or repeated exposure to conditions, which unexpectedly cause injury during the policy period.

Open Peril Insurance policy that protects the insured from losses caused by any peril that is not specifically excluded by the policy.

Other Insurance Condition Condition found in a policy that sets out how other insurance the insured may have on the same property will affect reimbursement under the policy when a loss occurs.

P

Package Policy A combination of coverages of two or more separate policies in one contract. Must include basic property and liability insurance. May also include various other casualty and property coverages.

Partial Loss Loss involving less than all of the values insured or calling on the policy to pay less than its maximum amount.

Participating Policy A type of policy which distributes to the policyholder a portion of the excess premium not necessary to pay for losses or other expenses incurred in the issue of the policy. Normally issued by mutual companies.

Payment Plans Various convenient plans for paying premiums by installments. Not available on all policies.

Peril This term refers to the causes of possible loss, such as fire, windstorm, explosion, etc.

Personal Lines Insurance coverages that protect individuals and their families.

Physical Hazard A hazard which is created by the condition, occupancy, or use of the property itself.

Policy The document issued to the insured by the company; the policy states the terms of the insurance contract.

Power of Attorney The written instrument by which the authority of one person to act in the place and instead of another as attorney-in-fact is set forth. Authority given a person or corporation, called an attorney-in-fact, to act for and obligate another to a specified extent.

Preferred Risk A class of risk considered to be particularly desirable.

Premium An amount of money paid to an insurance company in return for insurance protection.

Premium Notice A reminder sent to policyholders by an insurance company to give notice of the approaching date of a premium payment.

Producer An insurance salesperson; i.e., an agent or a broker.

Prohibited Risk A risk which a company will not insure.

Proof of Loss A statement signed by the policyholder making formal claim against the company for damage to or loss of the property insured.

Property Damage A coverage protecting the legal liability of the policyholder for damage on account of injury to, or destruction of, property, subject to certain exclusions.

Property Insurance Insurance which generally protects the personal property of the individual. Fire insurance is one example.

Property Losses Losses an individual might suffer which can be characterized as loss of the article itself, loss of income from the use of the property, or extra expense incurred due to loss of property.

Pro-Rata Cancellation A system of canceling a policy before it expires and returning to the policyholder an amount of premium proportional to the unexpired days of the policy. Cancellation by the insurance company.

Pure Risk A risk that involves the possibility of loss only, not the possibility of gain.

Q

Quotation An approximation of the premium for a given policy.

R

Rate The premium charge for specific coverage for the regular policy period. The cost of a unit of insurance for a specified period of time.

Rating The determination of the premium to be charged for coverage on a risk. Based upon risk characteristics and the actuarial calculations regarding the chance of loss.

Rebating The granting of any form of inducement, favor or advantage in cost or benefit to the purchaser of a policy not available to all under the standard policy terms. Rebating in some states is a penal offense for which both the agent and the person accepting the rebate can be punished by fine or imprisonment, with the agent also subject to revocation of license.

Reciprocal Insurance Insurance provided by subscribers at a reciprocal exchange. Each subscriber agrees to become liable for a portion of the losses and expenses of all subscribers and authorizes the attorney-in-fact to effect this exchange of insurance with the other subscribers.

Reimbursement Recovered payments-in-error, overpayments or contributions from a third party or his or her insurance company which are credited to the coverage involved in a claim originally paid.

Reinsurance Acceptance by an insurer, called a reinsurer, of all or part of the risk of loss of another insurer.

Rejection The refusal of an application for insurance.

Release Written acknowledgment stating that all obligations past, present, or future arising out of a particular accident or occurrence have been fulfilled. Signing by the claimant generally relieves the company and insured of any further obligation.

Renewal Continuation of an insurance contract beyond the original date of expiration, by endorsement, certificate or new contract.

Renewal Certificate A certificate indicating that a policy has been renewed or extended for another term.

Replacement Cost Coverage of household destruction up to the policy face value, with no deduction for depreciation. This is generally included in a homeowners-type policy, or may be added to a fire policy.

Representations Statements an applicant believes to be true. Compare to Warranty.

Reserve A sum set aside to meet future obligations. Amount of reserve varies with different types of claims as well as with differences in severity of claims.

Return Premium A refund to the policyholder, caused by cancellation, rate reduction, reduction in amount of insurance, or similar reasons, of part of the premium previously paid.

Rider Synonymous with Endorsement. Common to life insurance, but in fire-casualty normally used in the Bond Department only.

Risk

1. Any chance of loss.
2. The individual or property to which the insurance policy relates.
3. Technically, the degree or percentage of chance that a given contingency will occur.
4. The odds.
5. A peril insured against.
6. The subject of insurance, whether a person or thing.

S

Salvage The property in which an insurance company secures an ownership interest as a result of paying a claim for total loss or damage based on the true value of the property in its undamaged state or before the loss occurred.

Short Rate A method of figuring the return premium when a policy is canceled by the insured. A portion of the unearned premium is kept by the company for expenses.

Short Term A policy term of less than one year.

Special Risk Risks of a certain type or amount of premium. Normally includes all risks developing over $10,000 year-end premium.

Specified Peril *See* Named Peril.

Speculative Risk A risk that involves the possibility of either gain or loss.

Spread of Risk An insurance theory which states that an insurance company should *not* insure great numbers of property in concentrated areas. Helps to avoid catastrophic losses.

Stated Amount of Coverage A certain amount of policy limit, written in the policy, as opposed to actual cash value. Under such a policy the company pays the actual cash value, but not more than the amount stated, in the event of a total loss.

Stock Company A form of insurance company organization with the following characteristics:

1. The company is owned by the stockholders.
2. Dividends are returned to the stockholders.
3. Stockholders elect the management of the company.
4. A policyholder does *not* need to be a stockholder to purchase insurance.

Subrogation The transfer of one person's lawful claim, demand or right to another person or company. In the case of insurance, this principle of law has been incorporated in all policies. The insurance company, upon payment of a loss to the insured, is entitled to the insured's legal and equitable rights against third parties. These rights are only those related to the loss, and the company is only entitled to the extent of the loss payment.

Suspense A term used when correspondence is placed in abeyance for a specified number of days or placed in a file for reference at a later time, so that the originator can again write the addressee if previous correspondence has not been answered.

T

Total Loss

1. Loss to the insured of the entire value of goods or other property by destruction, damage, or deprivation.
2. Loss entailing the payment of the face amount of an insurance contract.
3. Property damaged to the extent that the cost of repairs exceeds the market value less the salvage value.

Twisting The practice of using misrepresentations to induce a policyholder in one company to lapse, forfeit or surrender insurance for the purpose of taking out a policy in another company. It is generally classified as a misdemeanor.

U

Unauthorized Insurer An insurer which is not authorized to do business in a given state.

Underwrite To scrutinize a risk and decide on its eligibility for insurance. To insure.

Underwriter Individuals or corporations who insure. More commonly, officials of an insurance company whose duty it is to scrutinize risks offered for insurance and decide upon their acceptability.

Unearned Premium That portion of the premium which covers the unexpired part of the policy term.

Umpire When a company and a loss claimant are unable to agree on the amount of loss the company should pay, the terms of many policies provide that each party selects an appraiser. If the two appraisers cannot agree on an amount, the two appraisers select an umpire. The decision of any two is binding on both the company and the claimant.

Uninsured An individual decides to personally assume all losses. Does *not* have insurance protection.

V

Valued Policy A type of policy with an amount of coverage specified and agreed upon by both the insurer and the insured prior to a loss. This amount is to be paid in full in the event of a total loss.

Valued Policy Laws A law, in some states, which specifies that in the event of a total loss, an individual should receive payment in the full amount of the policy, regardless of the theory of indemnification.

Vandalism Damage done maliciously. Also called "malicious mischief."

W

Waiver The agreement not to enforce a right or privilege.

Warranty Promise made by the insured in order to obtain the insurance.

Workers' Compensation Coverage required by state law against compensation to workers who are injured on the job, regardless of whether or not the employer has been negligent.

Writings The amount of gross premiums that is written.

Written Premium The entire amount of premium written by an insurer.

Index

A

Accounting Department 81
Actual Cash Value (ACV) 109
Actuary 73
Adjuster 53
Administrative Assistant 62
Admitted Insurer 47
Advertisements 57
Advertising Injury 103
Agent 53, 57–58
Aggregate Limit 99
Aleatory Contract 89
Alien Insurer 49
All Risk Policies 102
Application 59, 108
Apportionment 116
Appraisal Condition 116
Arbitration Condition 116
Assignment Condition 109
Attorney 83
Audited Premium 76
Authorized Insurer 47

B

Binder 60
Blanket Insurance 99
Bodily Injury (BI) 103
Boiler And Machinery Coverage 137
Bookkeepers 81
Broker 53, 58–60
Building And Maintenance
   Department 84
Bureau Adjuster 79
Businessowners Policies 143

C

Cancellation 105
Capital-Stock Companies 41
Casualty Insurance 38
Catastrophic Losses 5, 29, 104
Cause Of Loss 66
Ceding Company 70
Certificate Of Authority 47
Claim Representatives 53, 78
Claims 62, 77, 85, 155
Class Rating 71

Coinsurance Condition 111
Collision Coverage 125
Combined Ratio 155
Commercial Auto Coverage 138
Commercial Crime Coverage 135
Commercial General Liability
   Coverage 132
Commercial Inland Marine Coverage 139
Commercial Lines 91
Commercial Package Policy (CPP) 94, 130
Commercial Property Coverage 131
Commercial Umbrella Liability 143
Company Authorization 47
Comprehensive Coverage 126
Concealment 107
Conditions 97, 105
Consequential Loss 102
Consideration 88
Continuing Service 61
Contract Of Adhesion 89
Countersignature 61
Crop-Hail Policy 135
Customer Service Representative 62

D

Data Processing 84
Declarations 95, 98, 113
Deductible 113
Definition Of Insurance 18
Department 84
Direct Loss 102
Direct Response Companies 57
Director of Insurance 46
Dividend 92
Dividends 42
Domestic Company 48
Draft Authority 62
Duties Following Loss 109
Dwelling Policies 122

E

Earned Premium 75, 155
Earthquake Insurance 126
Easy-To-Read Policies 52, 91
Effective Date 98
Employment Practices Liability (EPL)
   Insurance 141

Endorsement 97
Engineer 6, 81
Errors 141
Errors And Omissions (E&O)
   Insurance 141
Exclusions 96, 104
Exclusive Agents 57
Expense Ratio 155
Experience Rating 72
Expiration Date 98

F

Fair Credit Reporting Act 65
Farm Coverage 134
Federal Crop Insurance Program 54
Fiduciary Liability Policy 141
Field Claim Representative 79
Financial Regulation 49
Flat Cancellation 106
Floater 93
Flood Insurance 126
Foreign Company 48
Fraternal Organization 44
Fraud 107, 151–152

H

Hazard 66
Health And Disability Insurance 37
Homeowners Policy 93, 118
Human Resources Department 84

I

Indemnification 32, 116
Independent Adjuster 79
Independent Agents 57
Indirect Loss 102
Information Services 84
Inside Adjuster 79
Insurability 22
Insurable Interest 30
Insurance Commissioner 46
Insurance Contract 85
Insurance Services Office (ISO) 73, 90
Insured 88
Insurer 88
Insuring Agreement 96, 100, 102

Index

...sion Of Privacy 103
Investment Department 83
Investment Specialist 83

J

Judgment Rating 72

L

Law Of Large Numbers 20, 22
Legal Department 83
Liability 38
Liability Insurance 38
Liability Risk 16
Libel 103
Licensing Requirements 52
Life Insurance 37
Limit Of Insurance 99
Lloyd's Association 44
Loss Control 85
Loss Control Specialist 6, 81
Loss Costs 73
Loss Payable Clause 114
Loss Payee 114
Loss Prevention 7, 17, 81
Loss Ratio 155
Loss Reserve 80

M

Mail Operations Department 84
Major Branches Of Insurance 36
Malpractice Insurance 133
Managing Risk 17
Manual Rating 71
Market Value 110
Material Fact 108
Merit Rating 72
Minimum Premium 74
Misrepresentation 53, 107
Mobile Home Insurance 126
Monoline Policies 94
Moral Hazard 67
Morale Hazard 67
Mortgage Clause 114
Mortgagee 114
Multiline 94
Mutual Companies 42

N

Named Insured 98
Named Peril 101
National Flood Insurance Program 54
Negligence 38

Nonaccidental Losses 104
Nonadmitted Insurer 47
Nonparticipating Policies 91
Nonpayment Of Premium 106
Nonrenewal 107
Nonreporting Policies 93

O

Ocean Marine 143
Office Adjuster 79
Office Manager 62
Open Perils 102
Other Insurance Condition 115
Other Than Collision (OTC) Coverage 126
Outside Adjuster 79

P

Package Policies 94
Participating Policies 91
Peace Of Mind 89, 147
Peril 6, 66, 100
Personal Auto Policies 126
Personal Injury 103
Personal Inland Marine 126
Personal Lines 91, 94
Personal Risk 15
Personal Umbrella Liability Insurance 127
Personal Watercraft Insurance 127
Personnel 84
Physical Damage Coverages 125
Physical Hazard 67
Policy Analyst 77
Policy Issue Clerks 77
Policy Period 98
Policy Term 98
Policy Typist 77
Premium 19, 59, 64, 71, 88
Premium Auditor 76
Premium Taxes 9
Principle Of Indemnity 32, 92
Pro Rata Premium Refund 106
Producer 53
Professional Liability Insurance 140
Proof Of Loss 109
Property Damage (PD) 103
Property Insurance 37, 93
Property Risk 16
Provisional Premium 76
Public Adjuster 79
Public Awareness 7
Punitive Damages 33
Pure Risk 29, 148

Q

Quotation 59

R

Rate Regulation 50
Rater 85
Rating Methods 71
Reciprocal Companies 43
Reinsurance 69
Reinsurer 70
Replacement Cost 110
Reporting Policies 93
Representations 108
Reserving 80
Risk 14, 64, 149
Risk Reduction 17

S

Sales 57, 85
Scheduled Insurance 99
Screener 77
Separate Limits 99
Short Rate Cancellation 106
Simplified Policies 90
Single Limit 99
Slander 103
Special Coverage 102
Specified Peril 101
Speculative Risk 29, 148
Spread Of Risk 22
Staff Claim Representative 79
Standard Policy 52, 73, 77, 90–91, 97
State Of Domicile 48
State Regulation 46
Stock Companies 41
Subrogation Condition 114
Superintendent Of Insurance 46

T

Teams 85
Technician 77
Telephone Claim Representative 79
The Government As An Insurer 54
Third-Party Losses 39
Time Element Coverage 102
Trade Practice Regulation 53
Transferring Risk 18, 19
Types Of Insurance Companies 41

U

Umpire 116
Unauthorized Insurer 47

Underwriter 64, 85
Underwriting Authority 68
Underwriting Manual 69
Unearned Premium 74
Unilateral Contract 89
Uninsured Motorists Coverage 125

V

Valuation Condition 109
Valued Policy 92
Vandalism And Malicious
  Mischief (V&MM) 100

W

Warranty 108
Workers' Compensation 54, 142
Written Premium 75, 155

Required Disclaimers:

CFA Institute does not endorse, promote, or warrant the accuracy or quality of the products or services offered by Kaplan Schweser. CFA Institute, CFA®, and Chartered Financial Analyst® are trademarks owned by CFA Institute.

Certified Financial Planner Board of Standards Inc. owns the certification marks CFP®, CERTIFIED FINANCIAL PLANNER™, and federally registered CFP (with flame design) in the U.S., which it awards to individuals who successfully complete initial and ongoing certification requirements. Kaplan University does not certify individuals to use the CFP®, CERTIFIED FINANCIAL PLANNER™, and CFP (with flame design) certification marks. CFP® certification is granted only by Certified Financial Planner Board of Standards Inc. to those persons who, in addition to completing an educational requirement such as this CFP® Board-Registered Program, have met its ethics, experience, and examination requirements.

Kaplan Schweser and Kaplan University are review course providers for the CFP® Certification Examination administered by Certified Financial Planner Board of Standards Inc. CFP Board does not endorse any review course or receive financial remuneration from review course providers.

GARP® does not endorse, promote, review, or warrant the accuracy of the products or services offered by Kaplan Schweser of FRM® related information, nor does it endorse any pass rates claimed by the provider. Further, GARP® is not responsible for any fees or costs paid by the user to Kaplan Schweser, nor is GARP® responsible for any fees or costs of any person or entity providing any services to Kaplan Schweser. FRM®, GARP®, and Global Association of Risk Professionals™ are trademarks owned by the Global Association of Risk Professionals, Inc.

CAIAA does not endorse, promote, review or warrant the accuracy of the products or services offered by Kaplan Schweser, nor does it endorse any pass rates claimed by the provider. CAIAA is not responsible for any fees or costs paid by the user to Kaplan Schweser nor is CAIAA responsible for any fees or costs of any person or entity providing any services to Kaplan Schweser. CAIA®, CAIA Association®, Chartered Alternative Investment Analyst℠, and Chartered Alternative Investment Analyst Association® are service marks and trademarks owned by CHARTERED ALTERNATIVE INVESTMENT ANALYST ASSOCIATION, INC., a Massachusetts non-profit corporation with its principal place of business at Amherst, Massachusetts, and are used by permission.

CPCU® is a registered mark owned by the American Institute for CPCU and the Insurance Institute of America.

ChFC®, Chartered Financial Consultant®, CLU®, Chartered Life Underwriter®, and CASL®, Chartered Advisor for Senior Living®, are registered marks owned by The American College. Kaplan Schweser is not affiliated or associated in any way with The American College. The American College does not endorse, promote, review, or warrant the accuracy of any courses, exam preparation materials, or other products or services offered by Kaplan Schweser and does not verify or endorse any claims made by Kaplan Schweser regarding such products or services, including any claimed pass rates.